Do It Yourself
BUSHCRAFT

A BOOK OF THE
BIG OUTDOORS

"FER IF THE LORD MADE FISHIN'
WHY—A FELLER OUGHT TO FISH!"

Do It Yourself
BUSHCRAFT

A BOOK OF THE
BIG OUTDOORS

DANIEL BEARD

Co-founder, Boy Scouts of America®

With 306 illustrations by the author

Dover Publications, Inc.
Mineola, New York

Bibliographical Note

This Dover edition, first published in 2017, is an unabridged republication of the work originally published in 1925 by J. B. Lippincott Company, Philadelphia.

International Standard Book Number

ISBN-13: 978-0-486-81619-7
ISBN-10: 0-486-81619-2

Manufactured in the United States by LSC Communications
81619201   2017
www.doverpublications.com

PREFACE

"The simple things, the true things" are not the products of urban life; they are foreign to the "great white ways" of the city, where art, science and crime have combined to make things wonderfully complex. There were no moon-faced, thick-waisted men among the George Rodger Clarks, Boones, Kentons and Crocketts. These wilderness men were tall, slender, lithe and athletic.

Robert Service's *Law of the Yukon,* where he so dramatically and forcefully shows that "only the strong shall thrive," has always been the law of the wilderness. But what Service has not shown, and what is equally true, is that the wilderness by its intensive training itself develops that very strength of character and strength of muscle necessary to survive. The Government of the United States was founded in the big outdoors, its front yard was the sands of the ocean, its back yard a howling wilderness.

The outdoor world has a way of its own of giving distinction to his devotees and all through the pages of history, from Christ himself to the present day, the outdoor man stands forth in bold relief. George Washington was a mighty hunter and a pioneer. Abraham Lincoln was a backwoodsman and a flatboatman, and Colonel Roosevelt was a conspicuous example of the outdoor man of to-day.

It seems to be absolutely necessary for the morality, the stability and the health of our nation, that our young people should have free access to the forest and field. A normal life is produced neither by the palace or the hovel—it needs the hot rays of the sun, the pelting of the storm, the bivouac in the wilderness, the climbing of mountains, "shooting the wrath of the rapids," in order to build up the muscles, the mind and the morals of a well-balanced manhood.

We must learn that education cannot be fenced in by the "three R's" or limited by Latin and Greek. The early Americans, clothed in deerskin garments, were often highly educated but lived scarcely less crudely than their enemies, the Redmen; but they were happy, they possessed in the fullest extent life, liberty and the pursuit of happiness which Jefferson tersely summed as the stimulus which causes human exertion.

The bald-headed, the spectacle-eyed man is the product of the city or of the indoor life; he is paying the penalty of breaking the laws of Nature by the loss of some of the normal attributes of perfect manhood. The thick waist and the short breath of the city man is the direct result of his artificial life; the lithe, sinewy, slender figures of the early Americans was the direct result of their life in the open. The author has seen a fat, pampered city dog thrown into convulsions by a short, strenuous run, yet the gaunt, lean wolves of the wilderness will run all day without tiring, and the gaunt, lean Americans won out when opposed to the well-fed, thick-waisted foes.

Which leads up to the fact that the author wants
to impress upon his reader and the public, that outdoor pursuits should no longer be classed as mere
sports but recognized as vitally important parts of
real education. The stifling walls of houses, the
weakening influence of ease and luxury and the
benumbing influence of abject poverty stunt, dwarf
and atrophy manhood and the normal development
of the five senses.

The big cities have no place for healthy, whole-
some happiness and the youthful joy of life. The
white light districts are only refined and luxurious
editions of the red light districts; there exists no
fundamental differences in the morals of either, and
real happiness cannot exist without rugged virtue
and vigorous morality.

It is the outdoor men like Abraham Lincoln,
Washington, Jefferson, Roosevelt, Boone and George
Rodger Clark whose names stand high above the
crowd in our own history; it is the William Tells,
Robin Hoods and Robinson Crusoes who hold the
permanent and prominent positions in folk-lore and
romance. It is men like Fred Remington and
Belmore Browne who distinguished themselves in
art; it is men like Audubon and Thoreau who leave
a lasting impression in the literature of the age. It
is the Buffalo Bills and Kit Carsons that appeal
strongest to our youth.

We all feel the effort of the inner-man to throw
aside the artificialities which impede thought and
action, and to seek fields of enterprise outside the
counting-room, the dusty library and the sweat-

shops of science and literature. Don't misunder-
stand, the author is a lover of old books and an
advocate of higher education, but he does not believe
the Lord created us to live the life of moles and other
creatures which dread the sunlight.

The writer hopes that he is doing his little
towards laying the foundation stone of the great
university of the outdoor world, which must soon
materialize in answer to the protests against the
devitalizing, weakening vices generated by indoor
life and imported by America from ancient and
senile civilizations.

The health and happiness of our young people
is absolutely necessary in order to produce normal
men and women, so the happiness of our young
people is the most important thing for the nation
and society to develop. Youth is by nature an
explorer, and an adventurer. From the time the
babe begins to creep up to the time that the adult
is chained to the treadmill of business or profession,
youth is constantly seeking adventure, seeking fairy-
land, seeking discoveries. Youth is inspired by the
same impulse which sent Columbus to America, Cook
on his voyages around the world, Stanley to Central Africa, Perry to the North Pole, Scott and
Shackleton to the South Pole. These aspirations
should not be stifled, the young people must have
access to the great outdoors.

DANIEL CARTER BEARD

FLUSHING, L. I., JUNE 3, 1925

CONTENTS

DO IT YOURSELF

CHAPTER I

FISHING
SUCKERS AND HOW TO KNOW THE SUNNIES
BASS DISTINCTION

> "I jes' set here a-dreamin'—
> A-dreamin' every day,
> Of the sunshine that's a-gleamin'
> On the rivers fur away.
>
> "So I nod an' fall to wishin'
> I was where the waters swish,
> Fer if the Lord made fishin'
> Why—a feller ought ter fish."
>
> —*Recreation.*

FISHING

WHEN we fished off the board rafts in the Ohio we fished for channel-cats, white bass, buffalo, and occasionally yellow bass.

When we fished off the log rafts in the Licking River we fished for mud-cats and channel-cats and caught many gars for which we were not fishing. When we fished in Bank Lick we fished for "Bank Lick bass," probably the calico or strawberry bass. When we fished in Brookshaws Pond and the other ponds in Covington, Kentucky, we fished for "pizen" cats, in other words bull-pouts.

On rare occasions we fished off the wharf-boat

1

where the ferry landed, just below where the suspension bridge now stands; there we caught splendid strings of jack salmon, known in the East as wall-eyed pike. Sometimes we caught "new lights," or crappies, a fish that was supposed to have made its appearance in that neighborhood at the same time as the people who called themselves New Lights.

We knew nothing about pickerel, trout or black bass. Some of them may have inhabited some of those waters but I doubt it; we never caught them and we never saw them even though the "little pickerel" are said to be common in the Ohio.

One glorious day my picturesque and distinguished daddy sold some paintings and I suppose that he felt rich; so like the real artist that he was he immediately sought some way of spending that money to delight his family and took us all up to Yellow Springs, Ohio, which was a paradise for any real boy, not the summer hotel where we slept and where Tom and I (sometimes) ate, but the glen with the aquatic plants and aquatic creatures. The Yellow Spring from which the summer resort derived its name boiled up in the centre of a pool and gilded all the tin cups and dippers with a tincture of iron which had the sheen and color of real gold, but that only possessed momentary interest for us, we wanted to get as far away from the summer boarders and summer hotel as our sturdy legs could carry us and each day saw us tramping along the shores of the streams and pools. Oh! those were glorious days and I hated to go to bed at night for fear I might miss something. I knew that lots of

interesting things were happening in the woods at
night while I was wasting my time sleeping in bed.

"The gypsy taint was in my blood—
The message cheats me still;
Yet I believe that Paradise
Is just beyond the hill."

—and we found it!

In the morning we were abroad at daylight and
as soon as we could get our breakfast we hit the
trail to Blue Hole, a delightfully mysterious pool
which nestled in the cleft among the rocks below a
picturesque old mill with a big water-wheel. Blue
Hole of hallowed memories! It used to be a wild,
lonely place, a canyon, the bottom filled with deep,
dark blue water. As I remember, the rocks on each
side were towering high. But, of course, the cliffs
may have shrunk since those great days when everything was big but me. Since then I have had many
occasions to remark that the big things that I saw
when I was a boy have shrunk very much in the
washing the years have given them, and some things
have even faded and lost color. It is a constant
source of surprise to me to find how narrow are the
streams which were once so broad, and it is shocking to discover that what were mountains to me then,
are only moderate-sized hills now! So this Blue
Hole may be now surrounded by comparatively low
banks. But, nevertheless, it was once a delightfully
dark, deep, shadowy chasm in the towering rocks,
and we felt that each cave and hollow must be the

"Our Man Friday Catamaran."

lurking place of Indians, bears, wolves, and panthers, or at least their ghosts.

Rumor said that there was no bottom to the pool, and we never doubted the rumor. I choose to believe it now, and I think I would be tempted to thrash the man who would try to shatter my faith and prove to me that Blue Hole really had a bottom to it like any other old pool.

Glory be to Peter! I believe that I can smell the pine, I can see the moss on the rocks dripping with moisture, the luxuriant growth of ferns, the old red fox stealing along the rocks upon the opposite side, and our Man Friday catamaran made of logs moored to the shore, the raft which we rowed and from which we swam and fished!

When I went swimming mother always used to make me promise not to "go over my head," and I religiously obeyed her commands; but somehow or another when we took our fishing-rods and went to Blue Hole she forgot to say anything about it. Tom was with me, and we dived into that deep water and swam around, experiencing a joy and happiness only to be duplicated in Heaven.

Under an overhanging rock, in awesome depths, lurked the biggest rock-bass I have ever caught, but we never took any fish back to the hotel to be spoiled by professional cooks. No sir-ree, bob horse fly—we cooked and ate those red eyes on the shore of the pool, where we learned lessons in the culinary art and fire-building which I have been teaching the boys and their fathers and grandfathers for the last forty-odd years.

Nature bestowed a priceless gift upon small boys, and big fishermen, when she endowed them with a wonderful imagination. Stop a moment and think. Did it ever occur to you that the gulf which separates a boy from a clam is not due so much to the difference in their forms as to the lack of imagination on the part of the clam? A clam never sits at his desk with his schoolbooks before him, dreaming of the trout streams; the parts of speech in the clam's mind never turn into bobbing corks; the lines of the printed book into rippling water. Why? Not because the clam is any better than the boy, but because the boy possesses an imagination and the clam does not. If the fish that got away was the biggest fish in the lake, in the mind of the lad who lost him, for goodness sake why not take his word for it. Tom and I were not clams, we both possessed imagination and we knew that some of the rock-bass we lost were every whit as big as salt-water halibut!

The Rev. Henry Van Dyke, in the writer's presence, said that the moral barometer was always low near a trout stream, meaning that fishermen's stories must not be taken too seriously; Doctor Van Dyke is a celebrated fisherman himself and he knows. Even the great Audubon did not hesitate to allow his imagination mill to grind recklessly when it came to fish stories, and he handed C. S. Rafinesque, Professor of Natural History, Transylvania University, sketches of fabulous fish which no one had ever then seen and no one has seen since. Rafinesque believed Audubon and gave names to these mythical fishes which you will find published in his *Ichthyologia Ohiensis*.

There was an old fellow at the mill who taught us how to make wire snares with which to catch mudsuckers (Figs. 1, 2, 3, 4 and 5). Tom discovered a

big mud-sucker in the bottom of a brook where the stream meandered through the meadow, so I fixed the copper noose on the short line to my pole and carefully slipped the noose over the sucker's head down to his fat waist without disturbing the stupid fish. With nerves tense and all excited I gave a mighty jerk, the noose came up in the air, caught on a branch overhead, but to our amazement it contained no fish. The commotion stirred up the mud in the bottom of the stream, and as soon as it settled we saw the poor old sucker cut as neatly in half as if it had been done with a cleaver by a butcher.

Since those days, when Tom and I had such wonderful times, I have fished from the Atlantic to the Pacific, from away up in the Hudson Bay country down to the toe of Florida. I have caught big brook trout, great Dolly Varden trout, gaudy rainbow and cut throat trout as well as the stupid brown trout and the lively, gamey, small-mouthed black bass —regular sockdologers of over six pounds—and also fish of less lively nature. But somehow or another, although I have enjoyed myself and enjoyed the open, the silence of the wilderness as well as the whispering of the pines, the talking leaves and the noisy roaring of the torrents—yes, somehow or another, to use a homely expression, the cookies never taste like those that grandmother made! I have used the fly, I have used bait, I have used all the different sorts of lures, and when bait-casting came in I took that up too; but the rock-bass, cat-fish, sunfish and mud-suckers caught in my boyhood days, gave me more delight than the biggest fish caught since then.

Once, however, when I was but five or six years old, I did catch a big fish. Waugh! it was only yesterday or the day before when, as a barefooted kid, I was up in the Western Reserve catching painted minnows with a hook made of a bent pin fastened to a line of thread from my mother's work-basket.

Then came the day when I was allowed to go to the shores of Lake Erie with my adorable daddy and big brothers, and have a real fishhook and a real line attached to a long bamboo pole. The hook was baited with one of the painted minnows.

At the end of the pier, where the water was deep, my daddy and two brothers were catching bass, but I was not allowed to fish there, where I was in constant danger of falling overboard, so I fished near the shore where the water was shallow.

Presently there was a mighty tug on my line, so strong a pull that there was serious danger of being jerked off the pier. I gave a wild war whoop and ran for the shore—feeling the fierce "joy that the caveman must have felt when he hurled the javelin"—jumping down on the sandy beach I cast aside my bamboo pole and waded into the water, pulling the line in hand over hand. In a minute more a small boy and a five-and-a-half-pound smallmouthed black bass were wrestling "catch-as-catch can" sometimes in the water and sometimes on the dry sand.

The noise of the battle brought daddy and brothers running to my assistance and the fish and line were disentangled from my legs amid many exclamations of admiration and surprise, for that bass was the biggest one caught that day!

Since that time I have had a modest share of triumphs, I have shot big game, caught much larger fish, and won some honors and all that sort of thing, but no triumph in all my life ever excited in my breast the sense of exultation experienced when that

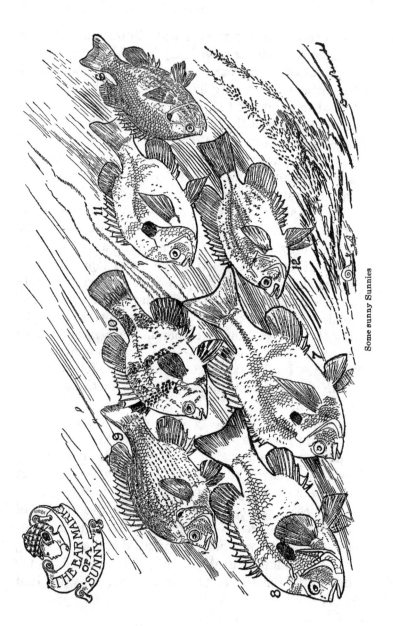

Some sunny Sunnies

five-and-a-half-pound bass was thrown flopping on
the sandy beach of Lake Erie!

"O Gee! I wish t'was summertime
So's I could use a fishin' line,
If this spring fever makes folks ill
Then fishin' fever's worser still."
                              —*A. R. Douglas.*

But big bass are not always to be caught by
boys, bass waters are not always within the reach
of boys. There are, however, many beautiful fish
which almost any boy may catch, and these in many
places are known as pumpkin-seeds. In Connecticut,
for some reason, the boys call them "roach" while
down in Dixie they are known as "perch" or
chinquapin perch. Sometimes the boys in the New
England States and on Long Island simply call
them "sunnies."

When my readers catch fish (they being more
intelligent than ordinary people and better educated), it is "up to them" to know what kind of fish
they are catching. Sunfish make a good pan fish;
they are easily caught, besides which, for their size,
they are very gamey and some kinds will jump for
the artificial fly as readily as a brook trout. Sunfish
are preëminently the boys' fish and they may be
found in almost any stream or pool inhabited by fish.

In order that the reader may pick out his own
sunnies, that is, the kind which inhabits the waters
which he fishes, I have made drawings of practically
all the sunfish known to me and placed them in one
group so that the reader may compare them with
each other and note the difference.

How to Know Sunnies

The pumpkin-seed sunfish (Fig. 6) derives its name from its shape. Any boy would probably call it a pumpkin-seed, but the scientific student of fish would call it Lepomis gibbosus, a terrible name for an innocent fish! These fish are plentiful in Wisconsin, and the lake at my camp in Pike County, Pennsylvania is full of them. They are beautiful in color and when taken small make a very good ornamental fish for the aquarium, and are vastly superior in intelligence to the goldfish. Pumpkin-seeds are very plentiful in New York State. Although they inhabit the coastwise streams from Maine to Georgia they are not found in the Mississippi Valley, except in the northernmost part. Therefore, Huck Finn and Tom Sawyer never experienced the joy of catching pumpkin-seeds. The pumpkin-seed in the big lakes sometimes reaches the weight of a pound and a half, but usually the fish caught are very much smaller. All the sunfish have a little dab of dark color on the point of their gill cover, as a tribal mark, brand or totem, and from its location it is known as the earmark. The pumpkin-seed has a rainbow-colored body and four stripes running across the gill cover, the two lower ones extending to its pectoral, that is, arms or front fins.

The Blue Sunfish or Copper-nose (Lepomis pallidus)

Is usually a larger fish than the pumpkin-seed and a gamier one (Fig. 7). Scientists call this one Lepomis pallidus. In Kentucky it is sometimes called the dollardee; it is also known as the blue green. You will find them from the Great Lakes to Florida, and from Florida to Mexico, and you can sometimes catch them weighing as much as two pounds.

The Long-eared Sunfish

The Lepomis auritus (Fig. 8), like everything else, is sometimes carelessly misnamed. But any boy who cannot tell a sunny when he sees it had better keep the pins in the cushion and not try to make hooks of them.

A glance at the illustrations however will convince anyone that there are many different kinds of sunfish. Among the tabbed fishes is the so-called Sacramento perch (Archoplites interruptus), of the Pacific Coast; the war-mouth bass (Chœnobryttus gulosus), found in our Southern States. The two last-named fish will be ranked by the boys with the rock-bass and red eye, but the others, the long-eared sunfish (Fig. 8) from the Susquehanna River; the Chinquapin sunfish (Fig. 9) (Lepomis punctatus) from Florida; the blue copper-nose (Fig. 7) (Lepomis pallidus) from the Tennessee River; the black-banded sunfish (Fig. 10) (Mesagonistius chætodon) from New Jersey; the rainbow sunfish (Fig. 12) (Centrarchus macropterus) from North Carolina; the broad-eared sunfish (Fig. 11) (Lepomis obscurus) from the Cumberland and Tennessee Rivers and the pumpkin-seed sunfish (Fig. 6) (Lepomis gibbosus) from the Northern States will unhesitatingly be dubbed as sunnies. Whether this agrees with the scientific classifications of the high-

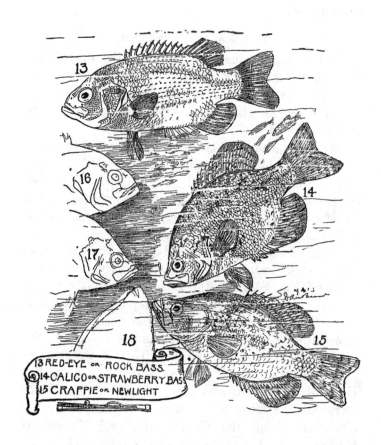

13 RED-EYE ᴏʀ ROCK BASS.
14 CALICO ᴏʀ STRAWBERRY BASS
15 CRAPPIE ᴏʀ NEWLIGHT

brows or not will not trouble the boy fisherman, for a sunny is a sunny and every fellow knows it.

There are a lot of small sunfish in the Mississippi Valley that Huck Finn and Tom Sawyer may have caught, and they may have called them "bream" or "perch." But the only perch with which the writer is familiar in the Ohio and Mississippi River Valley is the white perch.

Remember all those sunfish are branded with the dark-colored ear-tab and they also may be known by their brilliant colors and pumpkin-seed form. But they have some cousins which are great favorites with the boy fisherman too. Among these is the red eye or rock-bass (Fig. 13) dear to the hearts of boys, and the prettily marked and spotted calico or strawberry bass (Fig. 14).

Bass Distinction
The Calico Bass (Pomoxys sparoides)

Also called strawberry bass, is silver green, with dark spots unevenly distributed; mouth very small, general outline like that of sunfish, olive-colored fins (Fig. 14). This bass is sometimes known as the bitter-head and lamp lighter and Bank Lick bass. I have never tasted the head, so cannot tell whence it derived the name of bitter; we never caught it in the act of lighting lamps and we do not know why it is called the lamp lighter. I often fished in Bank Lick, but unless my memory fails me the fish I caught we called rock-bass which was probably a wrong name for them.

THE ROCK-BASS (AMBLOPLITES RUPRESTRIS)

Has an olive green back, sides coppery-colored and scales with a black spot on them. The rock-bass or red eye (Fig. 13) is a bully fish.

Now if you look at Figure 14 you will see that it is marked very differently from Figures 13 and 15, also that the fins on Figure 13 are a different shape from those on Figures 14 and 15; again, if you will look at the outline of their heads (Figs. 16 and 17) you will note that they have a different profile. Figure 18 shows the profile of the three fish drawn together.

CRAPPIES

Figure 15 shows the Pomoxys annularis. These fish are generally known as crappies, that is, along the Mississippi Valley; but in other places they have nicknames and in the Ohio Valley they are called new lights. The reason of this is because they made their appearance there at the same time as did the religious sect known as New Lights, at least, that is the legend, and people said the fish came from some spawn thrown in the Ohio River by these people. Sometimes they are called Campbellites and sometimes bachelors or sach-a-laits, but these are all nicknames; crappie is the right name and we will stick to that. In habits they are like the calico bass, but unlike it the crappies prefer muddy water.

The next time any of you fellows catch one of these fish you should at once be able to say positively, I have a red eye, a calico or a crappie, as the case may be; there will be no excuse hereafter for your mixing them up, although they have a general like-ness, and from their shape you may see that they are distant cousins of the sunfish.

In a chapter of this kind we cannot give all the fish—that would take several thick volumes—so we have left out the sunfish's cousins, the mud bass, the Sacramento perch and the war-mouth bass, all of which have the earmark of the sunfish but with bodies shaped more like the rock-bass and all of which are favorites with the boys in the states where they are found. These fish have even more or less faintly marked the dark ear-tab of the sunny. That earmark is either all that is left of what was once a stripe across the fish's body, or it is the beginning of a stripe that was never finished.

This chapter is like the ear-tab on the sunny; it's the beginning of an account of the sunnies which will never be finished, because this book is not confined to sunfish, however charming they may be, but is about the big outdoors of which the sunny is but a little part, an ear-tab so to speak.

CHAPTER II

BLACK BASS. PIKE FAMILY. HOW TO DRESS A
BONY FISH. HOW TO SCALE A FISH. HOW TO
PRESERVE A FISH SKIN. HOW TO MEND A
BROKEN ROD. TIP-UPS AND SPRING RODS

" 'Tain't no use to sit and whine
When the fish ain't on your line;
Bait your hook and keep on trying."
—*Ye Little Print Shop.*

Black Bass

Once upon a time, not many years ago, a party
of friends were visiting me at my log cabin on Big
Tink Pond, Pike County, Pennsylvania, the same
cabin which is now the administration building of
the Dan Beard Outdoor School. But at that time
it served no other purpose than a vacation abode for
my family and friends. All of our guests had been
fishing that day and all of them had good luck and
the host's turn had come. Leaving the happy guests
sorting their fish on the bank, I leisurely pulled down
to the lower end of the pond, near the outlet; reaching a point where the lily pads extend in a peninsula
almost to the centre of the lake, I allowed my boat
to drift while my line trailed out a long distance
behind. In a few minutes I had a strike and after
a great fight landed a five-and-three-quarter-pound
bass! My, my, he was a beauty! The line had
scarcely straightened out after the second cast when
I hooked a four-and-a-half-pound pickerel. This

18

was great fishing, but it is not what I started to
tell you about.

Swinging around so as to slowly return, I got
another strike and landed the funniest short humped-
back bass I ever saw. The three fish being more
than enough, I returned to the landing but in place
of being received by acclamations of astonishment

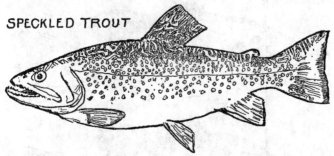

SPECKLED TROUT

and pleasure by my guests I was shocked by their
hilarity. Much to my discomfort and chagrin, both
ladies and gentlemen were convulsed with merri-
ment and before they could stop laughing and talk
I saw that they ignored my record catch and were
pointing at the humped-back bass, and then they all
began shouting, "He's got it, he's got it!" They did
not seem to see my two royal big fish, which were
the biggest ones caught that season.

It developed later, however, in the course of con-
versation that everyone in that party had caught
that same humped-back bass and because of its
ungainly shape had each thrown it back again. I
tell this story to show that a fish is not very badly
frightened when it is caught and that unless it swal-
lows the hook, or the hook becomes foul of its gills,

it apparently feels no pain. Another thing, this incident demonstrates that when a fish is hungry it is not to be discouraged from seeking its prey because of a few trifling accidents.

But when a bass *is not hungry* it is one of the most difficult things in the world to entice it to eat.

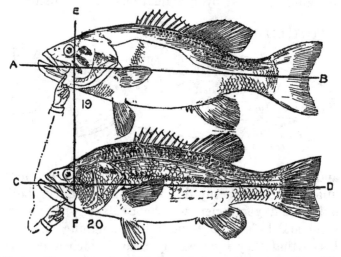

From the pier in the crystal waters of the St. Lawrence River, near the Thousand Isles, I once saw a large bass fifteen or twenty feet below the surface. I dangled my lure in front of his nose, he backed away; I baited my hook with a minnow, it had the same effect. I tried angle-worms, crawfish, bugs and beetles, I tried every sort of bait I could lay my hands on, and even dragged the baited hook across the fish's nose, but it would not touch it. The bass was not frightened because it did not leave the spot, it simply back-paddled away from the object which annoyed it. None of the arts of fishing, with which I was acquainted, could induce that fool bass to take the hook. It did not want to feed and it would not try. Such whims of the fish lend interest and charm to the sport of angling.

There are two kinds of black bass, the small-mouthed (Fig. 19) which is the delight of all fishermen and the big-mouthed (Fig. 20) which is also a good fish to catch but has neither the brains nor the staying qualities of his brother. The small-mouthed bass fights to the last minute; the big-mouthed will dive down and wind one's line around a root and sulk, but when put in the pan it makes better food than its livelier brother.

THE SMALL-MOUTHED BLACK BASS
(MICROPTERUS DOLOMIEI)

Is black and yellowish green (Fig. 19); its sides have a brownish yellow color. When caught and taken from the water the color rapidly changes and dark upright bars come and go across the body. The belly is white and the mouth, as you may see from the diagram, barely reaches to a point just below the eye, the scales are rather small, there are several stripes on the gill cover.

THE LARGE-MOUTHED BLACK BASS
(MICROPTERUS SALMOIDES)

Has a dark-green-colored back (Fig. 20), sides a glistening silvery green, white belly and faint stripes running from the gill cover to the tail. The big mouth extends to a point beyond the eye, as may be seen in Figure 20.

In Figures 19 and 20 the lines A–B and C–D are supposed to run through the centre of the fish and the line E–F at right angles or square with the other two lines. This gives the relative size of the mouths.

You will see that in the large-mouthed black bass (Fig. 20) there is a faint indication of the earmark extended to a stripe reaching all the way to its tail. But the large-mouthed and small-mouthed bass have bodies much more slender than the sunfish or their cousins, the red eye, the calico and the crappie.

THE PIKE FAMILY

To many full-grown men the wall-eyed pike, pickerel, muskellunge and the pike all look alike, but they are not alike, except in the general form of their bodies, as a glance at Figures 21, 22, 23, 24 and 25 will show you. In the first place the jack salmon or the wall-eyed pike is neither a salmon nor a pike but belongs to the perch family. Examine the fins, on the diagram, of the wall-eyed pike (Fig. 22) and you will note, in the first place, that it has two dorsal fins, that is, back fins, one supported by ribs or hard spines and the other supported by soft rays like those of the bass and sunfish. But the pike (Fig. 23), the pickerel (Fig. 24) and the muskellunge (Fig. 25) each have but one dorsal fin composed of soft rays. You will also note that the "arms" of

THE JACK SALMON (STIZOSTEDIUM VITREUM)

(Fig. 22) are located immediately above its "legs"; in other words its pectoral fins (the fins nearest the gills) are above the two ventral fins. This

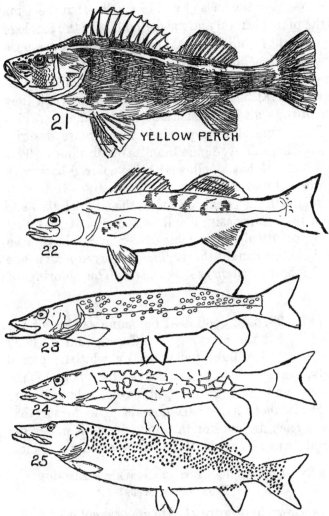

21   YELLOW PERCH

22

23

24

25

Perch Pike Pickerel and Muskellunge.

is also true of the bass (Figs. 19 and 20), but the arms of the pike, pickerel and muskellunge (or the forelegs if you want to call them that) are located about where forelegs of a land animal should be and the hind-legs where the hind-legs should be, that is the hind-legs (ventral fins) are much further back than they tive of the wall-eyed pike than its other names. This

The name of pike perch is much more descriptive of the wall-eyed pike than its other names. This pop-eyed fish has a yellowish olive-colored back with lighter colored sides and a silver belly. It is very abundant in the country around the Great Lakes and the Upper Mississippi and Missouri. It was formerly plentiful in the Ohio River and I have seen good strings caught there. The wall-eyed pike is one of the best food fishes we have. The coloring of

THE REAL PIKE (ESOX LUCIUS)

(Fig. 23) is a good deal the same as that of the pickerel, but the marking is different and its body is dotted with light yellowish or whitish colored spots, bean-shaped scales cover the whole of the cheeks, and part of the gill covers, the average weight is about five or six pounds. The dorsal, that is, the back fin, anal or tail fins (fin right under the dorsal fin) and caudal (tail) are spotted with black.

THE COMMON PICKEREL OR NORTHERN AMERICA (ESOX RETICULATUS)

Is shown by Figure 24. Its general color is greenish and it is covered with a sort of a chain-shaped, irregular markings, not spots like on the muskel-

lunge. The pickerel is a fresh-water shark in its
appetite, is not very gamey but usually of good size.
Compare it (Fig. 22 with Figs. 23 and 25), and you
will always be able to recognize it.

THE MUSKELLUNGE (ESOX NOBILIOR)

An Algonquin Indian told me that Maskinonge or
Maskenozha or Maskinoje (Fig. 25) simply meant
big fish and this Indian did not see the difference
between a muskellunge, a pike or a pickerel; they
were all fish to him but as a rule one was bigger than
the other. The muskellunge, as I choose to spell it,
is the Esox nobilior; it is the big fish we try to catch
in the St. Lawrence and sometimes succeed. Its size
is the only thing that recommends it to most fishermen. It is generally what the boys would call a
whopper or a sockdologer; it sometimes weighs as
much as twenty or thirty pounds. The back is dark
gray and green in color with darker spots, sides have
a tendency to yellowish green color, the belly is
either white- or cream-colored. If you hook one
weighing twenty pounds you will not have to examine
its gill covers for the narrow strip of scales in order
to identify your fish.

How to Dress a Bony Fish

With a sharp camp-knife cut through the flesh *to*
the ribs (Fig. 26) without severing them. Then
thrust in the knife at A (Fig. 26), and just to one side
of the back-bone. Cut the flesh from the ribs, being
careful to keep outside of them till you come to B,
where you push the knife clear down through, as

shown in Figure 26.   Next cut along the back-bone to the tail C.

Turn the fish over and cut the other side in the same manner, then you will have all the good flesh with scarcely a bone in it.   The slices cut thus when

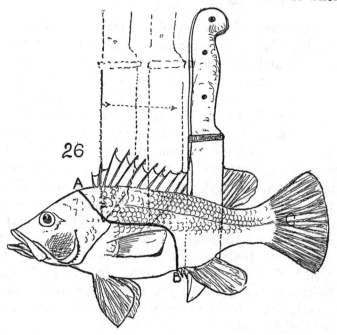

broiled crisp and brown will scorch any small bones that may still be in the meat so that they may be eaten as one would a bit of crust of toasted bread.

ANOTHER METHOD

With the back of the fish uppermost grasp it with the left hand, make a deep cut with a sharp knife on each side of the dorsal fin (back fin).   You can then take the fin itself out. Continue the cut, but now only *just through the skin* to the tail and then to the head. Take out the anal fin (belly fin) in the same manner you did the back fin, and also the two front fins. Next make a cut in the belly and remove the insides. Continue the cut, through the skin only, to the tail.

Next cut the fish through the skin crosswise back of the gill bone on both sides, but leave the head, the back-bone on until the job is finished when the back-bone with head attached can be thrown in the fire. Now place the fish on a stone or similar object and with your left hand on the head, press down firmly. Next get your finger nails under the skin near the back-bone, just in rear of the cut behind the gill bone, and pull the skin back toward the tail of the fish. Skin the other side in the same manner.

To take out the back-bone, place the fish down flat on its side and stick a sharp knife at the head end just over the back-bone and follow down to the end of the tail. Turn the fish over and remove the other side. You will now have two most attractive pieces of clean white meat. Quickly wash them and dry them without delay with cloth. Put them on a dry pan, clean chip or bit of birch bark and cover with fresh grass or sweet green leaves until ready to cook.

EASY WAY TO SCALE A FISH

Scaling a fish is ofttimes an unpleasant duty. A fellow from the Wooden Nutmeg State tells of a way to make the work easy. He takes a stick about as

large in diameter as ones little finger, sharpens it
to a point as one would a pencil (Fig. 27) and then
runs it down through the fish's mouth two-thirds
the length of his body (Fig. 28). This stiffens the
fish and prevents it bending and flopping about while
one is scaling it and "it is a joy to see how much
more easily the scales scrape off."

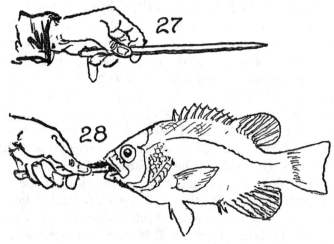

To Preserve a Fish Skin

Cut the fish about four inches along the belly—
skin loose from this slit up to the back bone and
work the skin loose from this slit up to the back-bone
and break the fish out through it, skinning it very
carefully to the head and tail, from which sever and
discard the body. The skin is then wrong side out.
Remove all bits of flesh and rub the skin with powdered alum (not salt), turn it right side out and sew
up the slit and the gills. Heat a pan of sand and

pour it down the fish's mouth, packing and shaping it with a stick to preserve the proper lines, sew up the mouth and lay the sand-stuffed skin out in the sun.   Next day it will be dry as a bone and may be perfectly mounted months afterwards.

To Mend a Broken Rod

Rods will break although it is usually the fish-

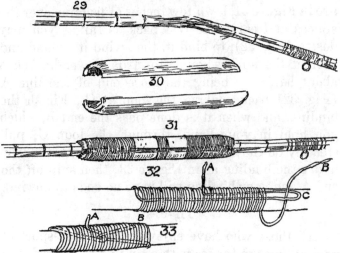

erman's own fault (Fig. 29), but such an accident can spoil a whole fishing trip, although it need not spoil your sport if you can use a pocket-knife and cut a few thin splints from a young birch, ash or iron-wood, or any wood that is handy.   Make the splints (Fig. 30) long enough to cover the break and extend beyond it two inches on either end.   These strips should be hollowed slightly to fit the rod and firmly wrapped in place with a bit of twine (Fig. 31).

Despite this slight bulge the rod will work nearly as well as before, although the "splice" will add a little weight. If the rod has "buckled" near the joint the repairs should be in the same manner, except the splints should be made long enough to reach beyond to the smooth ferrules, where they will hold.

To "whip" on the two splices (Fig. 30) as they are in Figure 31, lay a few inches of fish line over the splices and carry the rest back as far as you may desire (Fig. 32), to bind it, then wind it around and around the splices going towards the end. When about half way bring the loose end of the line A (Fig. 32) back, making the loop at C. Finish the binding, and when it is done pass the end B, which you hold in your hand, through the loop C; pull steadily on the end A until you have drawn the loop under the binding as in Figure 33; then snip off the end A and your binding will have no ends to unwind.

TIP-UPS

All those who have enjoyed the winter sport of fishing through the ice with a tip-up are enthusiastic over that method of catching pickerel. The tip-up used in winter time is made of two sticks, one stick to lay across the hole in the ice and another stick with a streamer at one end lashed on the first one crosswise, so that one end protrudes three or four inches on one side of the first stick, while the other end is a foot or more upon the opposite side; the streamer is attached to the top of the longest end and the fish line is attached to the shorter end. When

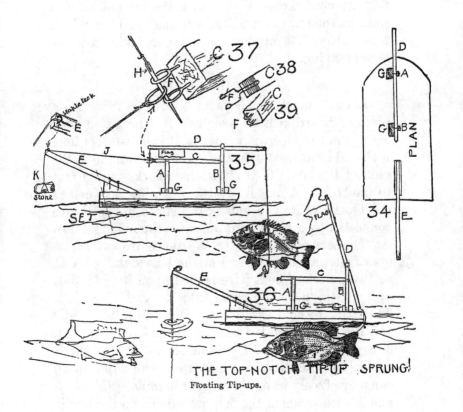

THE TOP-NOTCH TIP-UP SPRUNG!

Floating Tip-ups.

the first stick is laid across the hole in the ice, the
weight of the longer end of the cross stick, with the
flag attached, keeps that flat on the ice until a fish
pulls on the line; that pulls down the short end which
necessarily lifts up the long end and displays the
banner flying.

The Floating Tip-up

Is made on the same principles. First we take a
piece of board, a little over two feet long and wide
enough not to be cranky, that is, if it is two feet long
it should be at least a foot wide. Figure 34 shows the
plan of the boat; G–G shows two blocks nailed fast
to the board; A and B are two uprights fastened to
the blocks (Figs. 35 and 36). These uprights are
connected by a horizontal piece C (Figs. 35 and 36).
At the stern end of C (Fig. 37) there are two screw
eyes fastened into the end of the horizontal stick C,
or two pieces of bent wire lashed upon it (Fig. 38),
or two staple tacks driven into the end (Fig. 39).
These are to hold the trigger, which is a big needle
(H, Fig. 37) which is fastened to the tip-up D (Fig.
35). And now D itself is fastened to the upright B
by a pivot nail, that is, a nail upon which the tip-up
can move freely when the trigger is pulled; (Figs. 35
and 36) the moment the fish pulls down on the line it
releases the needle, which also releases the anchor-
rope J (Fig. 35) and allows the anchor K to sink
down and hold the boat steady (Fig. 36). The line J,
as you may see, is held in place by the trigger needle
H (Figs. 35 and 37) when the fish releases the needle
H, the stone or anchor K drops in the water and

FLOATING TIP-UPS

sinks until it is checked by the ring at the other end of J (Fig. 36). This causes the flag to fly (Fig. 36), and warns you that a fish is hooked to the line.

A Night Tip-up

Is made like the one above described, but it has no anchor and the trigger pin is attached at the lower end to a lantern, made by placing a candle inside a small tin box; a larger tin can is nailed fast to the float in which the lantern fits and hides the light, but the moment the fish pulls the trigger pin free it also pulls the lantern out of the larger tin pan so that the light may be seen from shore and the watchful fisherman knows there is a fish on the line.

Figures 40 and 41 are sketches of the night or lantern tip-up. D is the can for "dousing the glim," C is the tip rod, B the upright, A the block to which the upright is nailed, E is the anchor-rope. Figures 42 and 43 show how the candle-stick is made to fit tightly in the bottom of the lantern and support the candle with three nails. Figure 44 shows how to make the holes in the lantern, tin pail or can and Figure 45 is the finished lantern. Figure 46 is a detail of the tip-up.

Cork and Bottle Tip-ups

Figures 47 and 48 show respectively the bobber and bottle floats.

The Spring Rod

If you want to see a fish thrown clear out of the water it will be done when one bites on the line attached to the spring pole. Figure 49 shows the pole "all set." Figure 49–A shows how the tip rod is attached to the spring pole in such a manner that it works loosely on a nail. Figure 50 shows the trigger

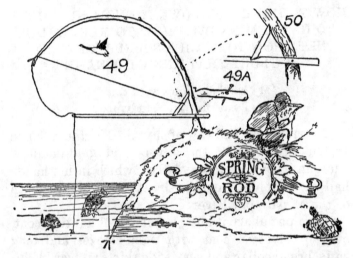

stick set in two notches, one cut in the spring stick and one in the tip rod.

When the fish pulls down the tip rod the trigger stick falls out and the spring pole suddenly assumes its natural upright position to the astonishment of the foolish fish.

CHAPTER III

HOW TO MAKE YOUR OWN MINNOW NET. HOW
TO CATCH MINNOWS. HOW TO MAKE A DIP
NET. HOW TO PITCH A SOURDOUGH TENT
A TROUT THAT KNEW HIS NAME

"My hand alone my work can do,
So I can fish and study too."

IN THE back hallway of my old Kentucky home
rested "Bald-face" the silver- and gold-mounted
shotgun belonging to my father, which in his hands
had won trophies from the Great Lakes to the mouth
of the Mississippi River.

On a peg above it hung a wonderful hunting-coat,
a drab velveteen coat with tight sleeves and long
cuffs, broad collar and very wide skirts; it was khaki-
colored and each bronze button had depicted upon it
a hunting scene, but no two were alike, there were
deer and quail, woodcock and bear. My word, it was
a wonderful coat, it had pockets everywhere and the
big wide pockets which circled the skirt of the coat
had dark sinister stains with bits of feather and hair
adhering to them; the big pockets were used as
receptacles for small game.

On the same peg where the coat hung, there was
suspended two leather shot-pouches with straps and
buckles forming a sort of harness to hang from one's
shoulders in such a manner that they partly circled
the waist, and their brass "chargers" hung con-
veniently at each side. Alongside of the gun, rest-

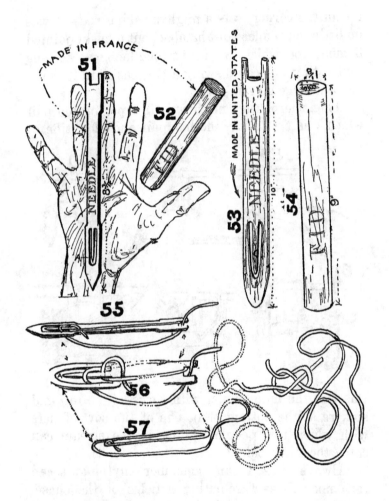

ing in the corner, was a mighty fishing rod—it was no little four ounce split bamboo, but a husky-jointed bamboo rod which, when put together, was so long that with it one could swing a bait easily to the middle of a large stream.

Then there was a minnow pail, a perforated pail which was set inside another pail and alongside of

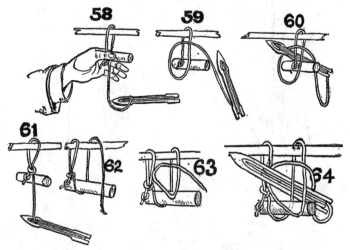

this was the minnow net with corks at the top and sinkers at the bottom of it, one of the sort of nets with which two people wading in the stream can catch the "live bait."

Always since I can remember anything, I can remember those fascinating articles of the chase, and the bronze powder-flask embossed with a hunting scene. There was and still exists an atmosphere of romance and mystery about these things that never ceases to appeal to my imagination. Many a time

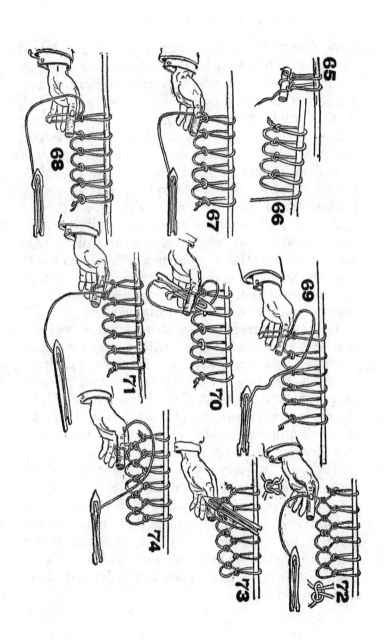

have I seen my father come home with a lot of
"painted" minnows in his minnow pail (the latter, by
the way, he made himself) or a string of four- or five-
pound bass and jack salmon (wall-eyed pike) which
he had caught by using his gigantic-jointed fishing
rod. Or I have seen him climb out of the wagon,
fire both barrels of the muzzle-loading shotgun, old
Bald-face, to make certain that the gun should be
empty, then blow into the barrels causing the smoke
to issue in two streams from the nipples, set the gun
against the white picket fence and pull from the
wagon a string of wild duck, an armful of wild
pigeons (now extinct), woodcock, plover, quail—Oh
Gee! and what fun it was to search in the pockets of
that velveteen coat, and how we feasted on the delicious game after grandmother had cooked it.

One cannot now take a short jaunt across the
field and come back loaded with game, but thank
goodness one can still fish, and there are still places
where one can catch fish. My father made his own
minnow net, minnow pail and jointed fishing rod, he
did not make his own gun, old Bald-face, it was an
imported gun with damascus wire twist barrels; it
now occupies an honor place in my studio.

There is no good reason why every one of my
readers should not be able to make his own minnow
net, and so I have filled the pages of this chapter with
illustrations and detail diagrams showing how to net
a net, depicting every position of the hand like a
movie film, and I want to tell you right here that I
would rather knit a dozen nets than to draw all these
diagrams over again.

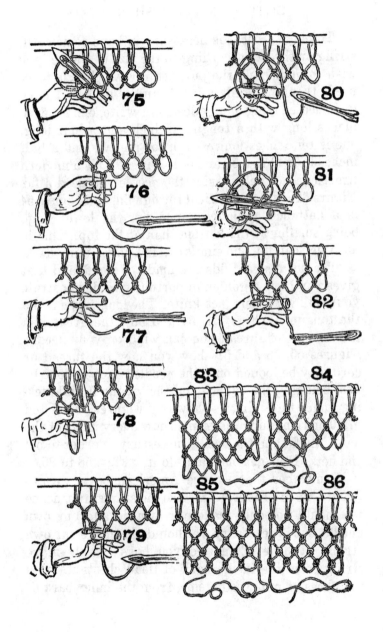

To make a net it is necessary to have some cord, string or thread, according to the size of the net you wish to make, and the purpose for which it is to be used; then one needs a "fid" and a needle. I have two needles lying on my desk as I write, one is seven inches long with a tongue an inch and a half long, one is ten inches long with a tongue two and a half inches long (Figs. 51 and 53). Figure 53 is a modern American needle. Beside the needle you need a fid. Figure 52 is the cylindrical foreign fid, and Figure 54 is a flattened cylinder-shaped fid, the lower edge being smaller at the bottom than at the top. This is an American fid, one similar to it I have on my desk.

The needles and fids are made of wood, and that gives you boys a golden opportunity to demonstrate your skill with your jack-knife. The longer you make the tongue A (Figs. 51, 53 and 56), the greater is the amount of thread you can wind on your needle. Figures 55, 56 and 57 show you how the thread or cord may be looped onto the needle which is done by first bringing the end around the tongue A and tucking under the string as shown by Figures 55, 56 and 57. The remaining diagrams show every move of the hand, the fid and the needle, necessary in order to net the net. Now get busy and do it. Figs. 58 to 86.

Remember that we are American boys, we are Scouts, we are Pioneers, we are the REAL THING, hence we should not only make our own fid and our own needle, but if necessary we should also make our own string. I have often told you boys how to make string from the inside bark of dead chestnut, from the fibres of milkweed stems, from the inner bark of the cedar and various other material to be found in the woods. We need homemade nets made by the boys themselves, of string of their own manufacture; we need a sample net at all scout headquarters where visitors may see what our American boys can do when left to rely upon their own resources, what they could do if they were left like Robinson Crusoe on a desert island.

There is no degree or scout merit badge to be gained by this but I'll guarantee the maker of such a net, be he scout or not, a letter from the National Court of Honor commending him for doing good work, signed by the Chairman of the National Court of Honor, and as many of his counselors as may be present at the time.

If the old Puritans and Pilgrims had known how to make nets, and how to use them, they need not have gone hungry; for there never was a coast inhabited by more fish, and a greater variety of fish, than the one on which these same pilgrims landed. Every Robinson Crusoe should know how to make a fish net, and so should every boy who reads Robinson Crusoe. It is a bully occupation when seated around the camp-fire at night, or on rainy days when one must stay indoors.

In order to go afishing one must "be prepared," and to be prepared to catch bass, pickerel, and other large game fish, one should have minnows. Of course, the tenderfoot *man* might think it necessary to pay somebody to catch them for him, but no real honest-to-goodness boy would want anybody to do it for him, for every boy knows that catching the minnows

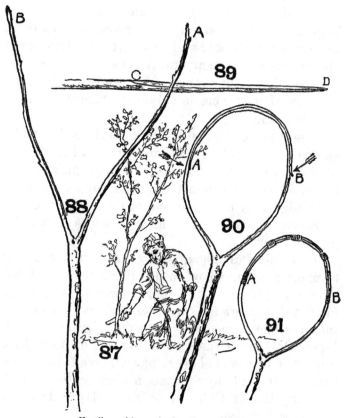

Handles and hoops for Landing or Dip nets.

requires considerable skill and is as much fun as
catching the big fish. I hope that all my readers are
the kind of fellows Horace Seymour Keller had in
mind when he sang:

"He fished for fish and talked to the birds
And I know they understood his words,
For they used to perch on a nearby limb
And cock their heads and listen to him,
Even the squirrels and chipmunks played
About his feet and were unafraid."

How to Catch Minnies With a Dip Net

There is more art and more skill necessary to
catch minnows with a dip net than a tenderfoot
suspects, one cannot approach a swarm of these
nimble little fish without great caution, neither can
one hope to make a quick sweep with the dip net and
land a single "minnie," these little rascals are too
quick for any slow moving human.

But with patience and alertness a boy or man
can soon fill his bait pail by the use of the dip net.
First scatter a handful of cracker, or dry bread
crumbs over the water at the spot from which you
have but just frightened the swarm of minnows,
then put a stone in your net for a sinker and allow,
if possible, the bottom of the net to rest on the
bottom of the pond or river, grip the handle of your
net firmly with both hands and brace yourself ready
for a quick upward swing of the net, but keep your
dry bread handy and every once in a while sprinkle
crumbs over the sunken net.

Sooner or later the minnies will return and when

great numbers are busily feeding over the net, steadily and swiftly bring the net to the surface. If this is done skilfully you will have the bottom of the net full of flapping little fish. If not done skilfully you will be lucky to have one minnie; but in order to catch the minnows in this manner you must have

A Dip Net

Because we like real problems, and just to make the problem difficult we will suppose that we have no iron ring or pole for our dip net; but that there is plenty of young wood growing near. In that case we select a tough young tree or bush (Fig. 87), cut it off near the ground and trim off the small branches leaving only the spreading forks (Fig. 88), these we carefully flatten on one side (Fig. 89), then we soak them in the water for a half a day so that they will bend easily without breaking. Next we carefully bend the two flattened ends until they lap each other as at A and B, Figure 90. All that is now necessary to finish our hoop is to lash the parts together as described in Chapter II, and depicted by F, Figures 32 and 33 of that Chapter. Our hoop will then appear as in Figure 91. Now take some fish line, twine or any sort of string in your possession and cut a number of pieces long enough and a little longer than will be necessary to make your dip net, festoon the hoop with these pieces of fish line as shown by Figures 92 and 93, then take the ends E and F, Figure 92 and tie them in a simple knot as shown by Figure 94, E and F, continue thus all around the hoop until all the strings are united. Next go

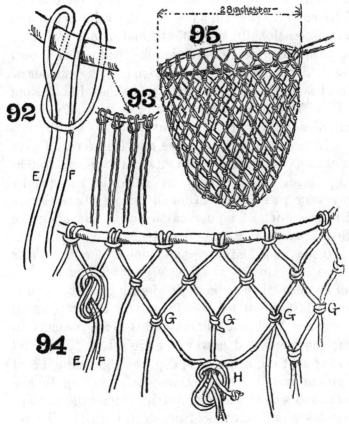

How to net a Dip net.

through with the same process with the dangling
ends as at G,G,G,G, Figure 94.

Of course, you will at once see that if this process
is continued you will have a cylinder net open at
both ends; to prevent such an undesirable result you
must occasionally snip off the end of one string as
at G and H, Figure 94, and make the knot as shown
at H. Thus one may gradually reduce the number of
meshes until they all meet and close the bottom
(Fig. 95); you are now ready to use your net to catch
minnies, killies, frogs, or crawfish.

In my book of *Camp-lore and Woodcraft* I give
diagrams of all manner of tents and manner of pitch-
ing them, but I have been called to account by
my very practical Sourdough friend, Mr. Belmore
Browne, for not laying particular stress upon the
Sourdough and Mountaineer tents.

Today when a fellow goes fishing, he really wants
to go out into the woods where he must camp, just
as he does when he goes out hunting for big game,
even if it is not necessary for him to camp, camp
"anyhow" because camping adds much pleasure to
the sport and that is what we are after. I am glad
to say that the American people are becoming a real
outdoor race. The most wonderful fishing I have
ever had was on a camping trip, among the unmap-
ped lakes and streams of northern Canada. Therefore, I am ending this Chapter with the two tents
which the famous artist, one of the first men to con-
quer Mt. McKinley, has pronounced the most practical tents for the real honest-to-goodness camper.

Of course, you know that a Sourdough is a fellow who has spent his winter in Alaska, consequently a Sourdough now means a veteran camper and is a proud title much envied by the tenderfeet. The Sourdough tent is the ordinary wall tent shown by

ON THE PLAN OF A CLOTHES LINE WITH TWO PROPS

97

96

THE SOURDOUGH SHRINKING OR STRETCHING OF TENT ROPES NEVER SLACKENS THEM

THE MOST PRACTICAL "PITCH" FOR A WALL TENT

Figure 96, but it is pitched in such a simple and scientific manner that it needs a special picture and description. Anyone who has had to get up in the night during a thunder storm and drive anew the tent pegs, which the tightening ropes have pulled from the wet ground, will recognize the advantage of having a tent so pitched that he may sleep comfortably no matter how hard it rains or how much the rope shrinks.

The Sourdough pitch for the tent is on the principle of a clothesline with two props (Fig. 97), the tent rope is stretched from tree to tree or from any objects which will hold the rope and propped up by a couple of shears, shears you understand are made of two forked sticks, set shear fashion under the tent rope. This supports the tent, then the tent ropes in place of being fastened to pegs are tied to a rather heavy pole, which is laid across the shears, a glance at the illustration will show you that this works automatically, that is, without any further attention upon the part of the camper. When the ropes stretch, the pole to which the ropes are attached slides down the shears without disturbing the tent. When the ropes shrink the pole to which they are attached slides up the shears and there you have it! A somewhat similar arrangement is shown in a small diagram in my other book. But I am glad that Mr. Belmore Browne insisted that I emphasize this very useful and practical tent.

The Mountaineer (Fig. 98), is the tent used by the Parker-Browne Exploring Expedition, amid the snow-clad highlands of Mt. McKinley, where they often pitched it on top of the snow itself. This they did by chopping holes in the hard snow with their alping axes, then driving the handles of the axes down in the holes, using them for the tent pegs at the four corners of the tent, which, after water was poured into the holes and frozen hard, made the

Comfortable and practical tents.

thing as solid as granite (Fig. 99). The Mountaineer tent has a floor cloth and an elliptical or egg shape opening, which is doubly protected by the tent cloth, which you see in Figure 98 tied up around the doorway, and a mosquito netting to keep out the venomous black flies, mosquitoes and other insects. The netting is gathered together in the centre with a pucker string, and can be opened, or closed at pleasure.

Now in regard to this mosquito netting, let me caution you never to leave it open. When I was up in the lakelands of Canada, the black flies were very thick and extremely annoying, so we ate our meals inside the tent and the Indian would open the pucker string just far enough to thrust in his hand with a pot of tea or with the frying pan full of sizzling trout, which we would quickly take from him and immediately close the netting as the hand was withdrawn. Thus we were protected from the flies while eating, and the nets we wore over our hats and the gloves we wore on our hands protected us in a measure from them while we were fishing. In that wonderful trout country where the trout frequently jumped out of the water after the flies on my leader, while I was busy attaching them to the line, they catch trout of great size.

The illustration (Fig. 100) shows an incident which occurred at the foot of some bad rapids around which it was necessary for us to carry the canoes, in other words to make a portage. The water was as clear as crystal, and from the canoe I could see the trout underneath the surface. As soon as I discovered that they were about to jump after the leader

100

which I held in my hand, it occurred to me that I would have some fun with our Indians who were squatting on a rock nearby, so imitating their French English I said to the Chief.

"Bow-arrow! Me heap big Medicine, ze trout, him know me, ze trout him know him name, him name Alphonse." Then dangling my flies over the side of the canoe, near the surface of the water, I cried, "Jump! Alphonse," and out sprang a trout. Again lowering my flies I said, "Jump Bill Smith," and no trout came. See I exclaimed, " Alphonse him know him name." Again I cried, "Jump Bill Jones," but no fish broke the surface of the water. The Indians were all attention and excited when I once more exclaimed, "Jump Alphonse," and immediately a trout sprang above the water after the dangling fly.

To use a boy's expression, "I put one over on the Indians!" And even the late Mr. Arthur Rice, Secretary of the Camp-fire Club of America, who was fishing from the rocks with the Indians, was mystified. But Joe Nipton, the Indian who was with me in the canoe only grinned. He was in a position to see how the trick was done. When I wanted a fish to jump, I dropped the fly within about three inches of the water, and held it there a moment when I did not want him to jump, I slowly moved it away so that the fish when he came close to the surface, seeing the fly was out of reach, did not break water. It is needless to say it was not the same fish each time, there was a dozen or more trout plainly discernible to the occupants of the canoe as the fish swam around close to the sides of the craft; but to this day if any of those Indians are alive they are telling how the white man knew the trout by name. Bow-arrow, Chief of the Montagnais, I am sorry to say, has gone over the Great Divide to the Happy Hunting Grounds. Our dear friend, and camping comrade Mr. Arthur Rice, has also crossed over the Great Divide where all the pony tracks point one way. We trust that over there he has met old Bow-arrow, the Indian, and that neither of them will be deprived of the joy of fishing the celestial trout streams where it will not be necessary to wear nets to protect them from the black flies. Honestly, I think the black flies belong to another region which we will not name.

CHAPTER IV

FLY FISHING
OIL BOTTLE FOR DRY FLY FISHERMEN

FLY FISHING
"Are you wishing
Jolly fishing."

SING the little yellow throated birds as they peer
at us through their highwayman's masks of black.
There is no use of us answering a question like that
and the yellow throats know it. At any rate, we will
allow the brown thrush to answer for us as he does
when he sings,

"Luck, Luck,
What Luck,
Good enough for me,
I'm alive you see."

I do not believe the Rev. Henry Van Dyke could
be the great fisherman he is if he could not also tell
us as he has, what the birds are singing. All good
fishermen must know the language of the birds and
be able to tell what is the gossip of the splatterdock
as it knowingly nods its yellow head above its round
floating leaves or the tittle-tattle of the blue pickerel
weed at the edge of the lake talking to the painted
turtle hiding among its blossoms. Yes, he must
know what the trees whisper, what the water is
laughing about and why the torrent roars.

First we catch minnows with a thread and a bent
pin, then we catch sunfish shinners, "pizen" cats,
next we follow the brook with a switch pole cut in
the woods, a short line and a hook baited with a
"fish worm" and secure a mess of real trout, that
makes us ambitious to become fly fishermen. We have
gone through the kindergarten and grammar school
of fishing but to win our degree of M. F. (Master
Fisherman) we must prove to be an adept with the
fly rod, but we cannot do this unless our hearts are
filled with the songs of the open, without which we
cannot enjoy the real thrills that the fish sends up
the line, along the rod to our hand, our wrist and
spine. Human nature dotes on thrills and they
furnish food for our nerves and our nerves demand
them! Not only that; but the boy who is denied whole-
some thrills seeks unnatural ones or relapses into
anæmic, cigarette-sucking, namby-pamby mollycod-
dle. Hence all boys are interested when at Sunday
School they read that Simon Peter said, "I go afishing," and they are in full sympathy with Thomas
called Didymus, Nathaniel of Cana, the sons of
Zebedee and the other two disciples when they cried,
"We also go with thee."

Of course, Simon Peter or none of the men of
his time knew anything about fly fishing, they used
nets and never discussed their preference for a dry
fly or a wet fly and there is but one way for us to
decide between these dainty lures and that is to try
them! You know a dry fly floats on top of the water
and an ordinary fly is not particular whether it is
on top or under the surface. When you have done

much fishing you will learn that some trout, like those in the Yellowstone River, take the fly best when it is under water, so we will not discuss this question at all. This is not a technical book on angling, no not by a long shot, it's a book of the big outdoors and angling only comes in for a share of the space because it is an outdoor sport and owes its position in the front of this book because this book, like the fishing season, begins with Spring.

The only way to learn to do a thing is to do it. In order to cast a fly, of course, it is necessary to have a fly rod (Figs. 101, 102 and 103), a rod with the reel below the hand and not above it; bait rods have the reel above the hand.

A Cheap Fly Rod

Can be bought at any sporting goods store, or department store, and such a rod is good enough for practice. One does not even need to have water to practice fly casting, but one does need an open space, free from brush and overhanging branches.

Don't forget that there are really only two movements, the lift and the cast. Figures 104, 105, 106 and 107 about cover the lift, the others, Figures 116, 117, 118, 119, 120, 121, 122 and 123 the cast.

The tennis court is well adapted for this practice. Casting the fly is principally done by the movement of the hand at the wrist joint (Figs. 111 and 112).

Hold the rod in your right hand with the thumb extended along the top of the rod (Figs. 113, 114 and 115). Assume an easy but erect pose with body and left arm perfectly still (Figs. 104 to 107). Figure 110

pose in winding up reel. Experts say that when the back cast is mastered all the rest is easy.

You need not put on a leader or a fly; but pull from the reel enough line to equal about one and a half times the length of the rod, and lay it out straight on the ground in front of you. Do not close your thumb on the fingers, but, as before said, extend it and rest it on the rod itself, as in Figures 111 and 112. Hold the line next its end in the left hand (Fig. 113) allowing the slack of the line to hang free between the tip of the rod and the hand holding the line.

How to Cast

Remember that in order to make what is known as a clean cast, your line must be out straight in front of you (Fig. 114), either on the ground or on the water. Now, with a sharp lift of the rod throw the line out behind you in the air (Fig. 115), in practice one may turn one's head to watch the line as it swings back. In the back cast the end of the line should not fall below the level of one's own head. To explain this we have made a set of diagrams on the order of moving pictures, of the positions of the rod and line (Figs. 104–123 inclusive).

The line is now back of you and even the rod is curved in that direction (Figs. 117 and 118). Bring the rod down now to the position of Figure 120, this hurtles the line out ahead of you (Figs. 120, 121, 122 and 123), and if carefully done allows the fly to alight lightly upon the water to be snapped up by the waiting trout, or to drop lightly on the practice field.

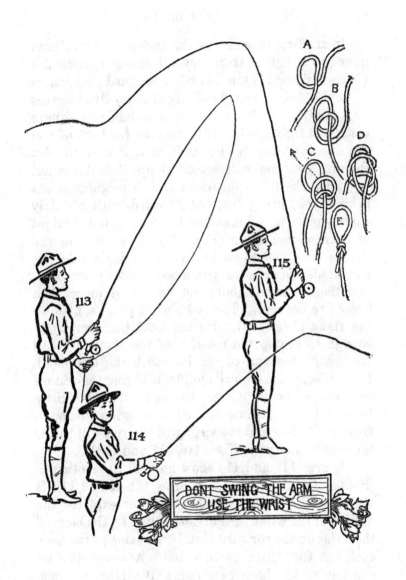

DONT SWING THE ARM
USE THE WRIST

In making these casts the rod should not have gone back but a trifle beyond the perpendicular (Figs. 116 and 117), nor further forward than where it would make an angle of about forty-five degrees (Fig. 123), with the ground, that is, half of a square corner or right angle. If it goes too far back of you the line will drop to the surface; if it goes too far forward your cast will be too "sloppy" on the water.

When the line appears to have straightened out behind you, bring the rod forward with a fairly snappy motion. This should lay the line out straight in front of you again (Fig. 123). The elbow of the casting arm should be held close to one's side (its a good idea to practice with a book under your arm), and the forearm should not be raised more than forty-five degrees. The rod should point a little to the right (Fig. 108). Do not hold the arm stiffly enough to cramp the muscles of the shoulder. As you let go the end of the line with the left hand, (Fig. 113), make a quick motion, bringing the rod up to a perpendicular (Figs. 106 and 107), or a little beyond it. This will cause the line to swing out to the front as it rises and the spring of the rod will throw the line behind you (Figs. 116, 117 and 118).

Figures 111 and 112 show how all the motion is practically in the wrist. Figures 111-A and 112-B show a wooden dummy which further explains the motion of the wrist. Figures 111 and 112, the bend of the wrist on the forward cast, is the same as the back cast but the action is reversed. A complete cast consists of the back cast (Figs. 104–116), a pause (Fig. 117) while the line straightens out in the air, and the forward cast (Figs. 118–123). The length of the pause depends on the length of your line.

Learn to make a pause at the back cast, long enough to allow the line to straighten out behind

you, otherwise you will snap the line like a whip, and snap off the flies when you are using them, or send it forward with a loop in the line. Practice will teach you to judge the pause, by the "feel" of the rod, it will then be no longer necessary for you to turn your head.

Practice on an open stretch of ground until you master the art of throwing the line straight out in front of you as in Figure 123. After you have managed this put a piece of paper or any other object on the ground and practice casting until you are able to make the end of your line alight steadily and gently upon the paper.

Try to make the fly or the end of the line hit an imaginary target about a foot above the water. This will allow it to drop like a feather at the proper spot. Do not forget that fly casting consists only of the "lift," which takes the line off the water, and the "cast," which shoots the line back again. Now get busy and learn the rest by practice. Do not allow the loop of the line to strike the ground before the end strikes the paper, for if this happens while fishing, and the fish are shy, the splash of the line will frighten them away, and if the fish are not shy, they may jump at the loop of your line instead of the fly.

Practice until you can cast gracefully, because grace in fly casting, or anything else for that matter, means skill. Let the spring of the rod do most of the work, the rod is made for that purpose.

Start to move the rod forward quite slowly just before the end of the pause, so that you can more readily sense the "pull." Do not try to cast more than fifteen or twenty feet until you can handle this distance with confidence.

About forty-five feet will be the longest cast you will need in fishing, and a good cast of six yards is

worth six poor ones of thirty. When casting begins
to tire your arm stop it. Practice often for short
periods. When you go out on the stream watch the
fishermen who cast well; you will notice they hold
the rod in the right hand (Fig. 108), while they pull

"Nonedohere
Osee·sWear;
Oachs·do·fray
Fish·away:"

·POSITION IN
LANDING A TROUT

some slack line from the reel with the left hand
(Figs. 108 and 109). With this slack in their hand
they can lengthen the cast by letting go the slack at
the proper moment and thus make the cast reach
the spot for the fly to alight. Do not be afraid to
ask them to show you how; all real sportsmen will

gladly lend a helping hand and all good fishermen
are sportsmen.

How to Join Two Pieces of Gut

So you have broken your leader? But don't try
to tie it together until it is well soaked and has
become soft and pliable. If you try to tie it while it
is dry and stiff the "gut" will break and you may
loose that big fish. As soon as the gut is soft and
pliable lay the two ends across each other as in Figure
124, wind them around each other as in Figure 125,
bring the loose ends around, bend them back towards
the centre, passing one under and the other over as
in Figure 126. Pull them taut and you will have the
knot (Fig. 127), which will not come undone.

But remember that while leaders are said to be
made of guts, guts are not guts, that is, not entrails,
but made of the silk of a silk-worm; however, everyone calls them guts and leaders and snells are made
of the material that is commonly known by that name.

Water Knot

Is one, if not the most important one to remember
when one wishes to join two pieces of gut together,
and it is one knot that will make a straight leader
without crooks or bends in it. With this knot, as with
all others tied with gut, it is necessary that the gut
should be softened in the water until it is perfectly
pliable, after you have succeeded in doing this, make
a simple half knot at one end of one piece of gut, and
thread the end of the other piece of gut through this
loop (Fig. 128), then make a knot on the end of this
one as you did on the first, the diagrams will explain

how the water knot is made better than my wording
can. Now draw the knots together and make two
half hitches (Fig. 129), draw these taut before you
snip off the ends of the gut, being careful not to cut
them too close. If you have in your fishing kit a
little copal varnish, a dab of it on the knot will tend
to make it more secure.

Loop at End of Leader

To make the loop in the end of the leader wind it
around, as in Figure 136. Bring the loose end down,
give it another coil and pass it under the lower loop
as in Figure 136–½, then take the top or left-hand
and bend it forward and over the lower loop as in
Figure 137, pull it through as in Figure 138, pull it
taut as in Figure 139, and your loop is complete and
ready to attach to the hook or fly.

Now that you have your fly or hook fastened onto
the snell (Fig. 131), and your leader fastened onto
your line (Fig. 130), it may be that you are a tenderfoot and do not know how to connect the snell with
the leader, but this is simple. You slip the loop of
the snell up over the leader (Figs. 132 and 133), then
bring the hook up and run it through the loop of the
snell. Pull it in place (Fig. 134) and your snell is
securely attached to your leader (Figs. 130, 131, 132,
133 and 134).

The Jam Hitch

Figure 135 shows how to make a simple hitch
which will often serve your purpose. It is known
among scouts as the weaver's knot, but among
anglers it is more often called the jam hitch. One

frequently uses large flies for large fish like bass and under such circumstances the fly may be too large to pass comfortably though the loop as the hook has in Figure 132, but this is unnecessary with the jam hitch (Fig. 135).

Oil Bottle for Fishermen

The real tenderfoot who has had no experience as a fisherman must not be frightened away by this black fly talk, because sometimes in some places one may fish in comfort all day without being tormented by the fly, as the writer has done many a day. But in spite of fly nets, dope and gloves, three weeks in the far North in June almost made a wreck of our party. We had bags under our eyes, one of the writer's ears was so swollen that it flopped backwards and forwards every time he walked, and the ends of his fingers were raw meat. This was all caused by those little black, humpbacked imps we call flies. One must cut off the ends of the fingers of the kid gloves so that one may be able to open one's knife, tie on a fly, and all that sort of thing, but the black flies are not slow to discover the unprotected finger tips and attack them, as pictured and described in our American Boys' Handybook of Woodcraft and Camp-lore. However, if you do not want black flies do not travel in the North; stay at home where there are mosquitoes because you know them and are not afraid of them.

"Fly dope" is that compound of greasy stuff that one dabs on one's face to keep off those terrible pests, the little humpbacked insects which breed in cool, running water and infest the neighborhood of trout brooks. The bite of this little Bolshevik feels as if a hot coal and a pinch of cowitch had been inserted under the skin. The best way to guard against black flies, mosquitoes and gnats, is to have netting fit over one's hat to one's shoulders where it is bound with a tape band. Also to take an old pair of kid gloves, cut off the tips of the fingers and sew chintz sleeves to the tops of the gloves to fit on the arms and be held in place above the elbows by elastic bands.

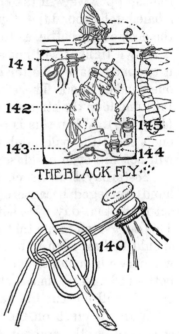

THE BLACK FLY

But "fly dope" is the generally accepted thing to keep these tormentors away, and, even when protected as described, the tips of one's fingers need dope.

You see those winged I. W. W's, declare that the Lord gave them suckers and the Lord gave you blood, therefore, they reason that their happiness depends upon free access to your blood and that they have a divine right to it.

Maybe the mosquitoes, black flies, cooties and Bolsheviks really believe in this sort of thing, but we who furnish our life's blood have other convictions; that is why we use "fly dope."

It is really too bad that Mother put our "dope" in a bottle with a glass stopper because the stopper is stuck fast and won't move; but shucks, the lazy-bird is singing—so in place of working too hard over that stopper we will take our shoe string and make a bale hitch around the stopper (Fig. 140), or around the neck of the bottle, as the case may be. When this is drawn tight it will not slip, but in order to cinch it one must have a better grip than is possible with one's naked hand. Therefore, get a small stick (Fig. 140) and loop the string around it as in the diagram, (Fig. 140). When this is pulled taut and grasped in one's hand the bale hitch can be cinched so that it will not slip even on glass (Fig. 142).

Yesterday I met a chemist friend who had one hand bandaged because of an ugly, long and deep cut made that day by a bottle breaking in his hand. This suggested to me that we must remember safety should be first even in balmy spring. Therefore, we will use our handkerchief with which to grasp the bottle (Fig. 142); then if the bottle breaks inside the cloth it will not cut the hands.

With the cinch on the stopper, or bottle, as the case may be, the stopper must be tight indeed that cannot thus be twisted loose and removed by turning the bottle one way and the stopper the other way.

But maybe in place of a glass stopper we have a cork which is anything but tight and there is danger of losing it and spilling the contents of the flask. In this case the cork may be made perfectly secure with a piece of twine (Fig. 144) which is made into a loop and then fastened by a knot, after which the

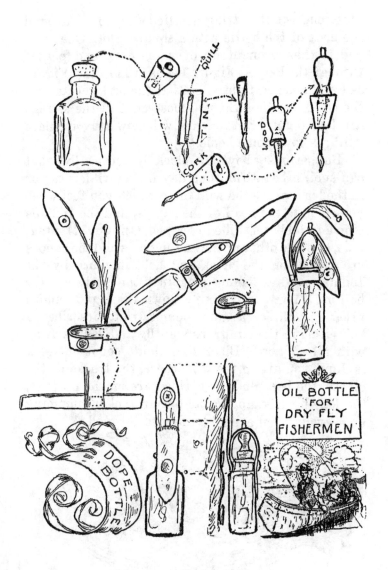

QUILL

CORK

TIN

WOOD

OIL BOTTLE
FOR
DRY FLY
FISHERMEN

DOPE
BOTTLE

loose ends of the string are tied (Fig. 145) around
the neck of the bottle with a square knot. One loose
end is then brought up over the cork and passed
through the loop A, Figure 144 as is shown by Figure
144 and cinched tightly, so that the string cuts into
the cork, and then the two loose ends of the strings
are tied together. The cork will now stay in place
"till the cows come home."

But seriously boys, the black fly doesn't live that
can spoil a beautiful June day in the wilderness or
in the least abate the wild thrill which you feel when
you come to the head of the rapids, and the Indians
stop and jabber a while in French, Ojibway, Montagnais, or some other unknown tongue, while the canoes
are poised on the brink and held in place by the
Indian paddles jammed against the rocks of the
bottom. You cast your fly down the rapids and a
great big three or four pound trout describes a
half circle in the air, grabs your fly and dashes away
with it! Whoo! Black flies don't count then—it
is June, you are in the wilderness, the tracks of the
moose, the bear and the caribou are on the portage,
the lazy-bird is singing and your reel is humming
and—well, "you are all willing to be good."

CHAPTER V

BAIT CASTING. HOW TO FASTEN HOOKS TO LINE
AND SNELL. SLIDING CORK. USE OF SAFETY
PINS. SAFETY CORKS FOR GANG HOOKS
HOW TO KEEP BAIT ALIVE

Bait Casting

One cannot be a real up-to-date fisherman unless
one is not only an adept at fly fishing but also at bait
casting. We have made bait casting follow fly casting
because the writer himself found it even more difficult than the former. Maybe the art is not so per-
plexing to others, but when the writer first attempted
it, it surely tried his patience to a degree that would
almost excuse the use of forbidden terms.

There is nothing more self-satisfying than to feel
the line run out smoothly, see the bait soar in a
beautiful curve and alight right at the proper spot
alongside the adventuresome lily pads, which one
will occasionally find ten or fifteen feet beyond the
bed of splatter dock, and which every old fisherman
knows shelters the favorite lurking place of that big
bass, the grand-daddy of them all, that he is after.

But there is nothing so aggravating, so tantaliz-
ing, so irritating as to have ones line back reel and
become tangled all up in the most complicated and
inexplicable manner, just at the critical moment, as
it certainly will do if the cast is not correctly and
skilfully made.

146

147

148

149

150

151

BAIT CASTING

For bait casting one uses a much shorter and stiffer rod than that used for still fishing or fly fishing. In selecting such a rod pick one about your own height (Fig. 146), also see Figures 158, 159 and 160. The whole art in bait casting consists in having a good reel and A GOOD THUMB (Fig. 147). I suppose you think your thumb is alright, but what I mean is a well-trained thumb. You will note in Figure 148 and including 153, that the thumb is holding what we term the spool (that is where the line is wound on the reel), and the speed with which the line unwinds from the reel when the bait is cast is regulated entirely by the pressure of the thumb. Figures 148–154 shows the short and the long hold, but this is a matter you must regulate yourself by experience.

Practise until you acquire the best and most convenient way of governing the line with your individual and particular thumb, which is different from any other fellow's thumb, because no two fellows' thumbs are alike. You need a reel that will run freely and smoothly (Fig. 160), not necessarily a very expensive reel, but it should be what is known as a multiplying reel, a quadruple multiplier is best. Keep this in good order, take it apart, clean it and oil it and be as careful of it as you would be of your watch. Use a line about twelve pound breaking weight, do not try a clumsy line, but one that will work free, and, if you are a real fishermen you will take great care of your line and dry it after each day's fishing, nobody but a dub, a tenderfoot, cheechako will leave a wet line on a reel all night. Such treatment rots the best of lines.

Some experts use what is known as a soft silk line. When you have your tackle ready, attach a small object to the end of the line weighing about a half an ounce, hold the rod securely, but do not grab it as if you were trying to squeeze the juice out of the butt, hold it firmly and naturally. Allow about ten inches of line, with the weight attached, to dangle from the end of the rod. Keep the padded part of

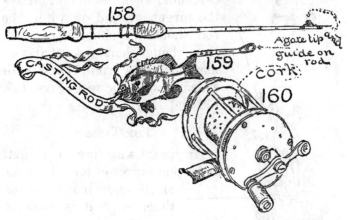

your thumb tip pressed firmly on the spool and bring the rod back over your shoulder until your thumb is about opposite your ear (Fig. 161), or your wrist in line with your nose, and the rod horizontal. Now bring your rod up with an even quick swing, start with a wrist movement (Fig. 162), and finish with wrist and forearm, the forearm aiding the wrist in speeding up the movement to the end (Fig. 163). The thumb gradually lessens its pressure on the spool, as the rod rises and is probably at its least pressure when the rod is in position of Figure 162, which allows the rod to cast the weight forward just as one throws an impaled potato from the end of a stick.

When the weight has almost reached its highest point of the cast, gradually increase the thumb pressure; as the line runs out the rod is lowered with the tip point following the weight at the end of the line as the latter descends, when the weight strikes the target, ground or water, the rod should be about horizontal, then change hands so that you may use your right hand with which to wind the reel (Figs. 155, 156 and 157).

THE TARGET

In practising use a target, make this target of a dark object on the snow if it is winter time, or if it is summer time, peg down three pieces of newspaper about the size of dinner plates, one at twenty-five feet, one at fifty feet and one at seventy-five feet from the tawline where you stand, and practise until you can make your lure alight on the targets. When you can strike the seventy-five foot target with some degree of certainty, you can trust yourself on the lake, river or pool with a real lure and the feeling that you are going to hook a real fish.

Don't be discouraged when your line overruns or back reels and becomes tangled. If this does not happen on your first attempt it will be because you are a natural born phenomenal bait caster, but it *will* occur, and you may have to borrow a hairpin and work a half hour on the line to untangle it. I have had to do that with a big fish floundering around the end of the line, and he "got loose" before the line did. The cause of this is improper thumbing of the line, the line was allowed to run out too suddenly.

When the weight is over the target check the reel by pressing the thumb lightly on the spool of the reel, which will stop the weight and allow it to drop without too much force, upon the target. Just as the bait strikes elevate the tip of the rod a trifle, then begin to reel in, for, in order to catch fish, the lure must be constantly moving and look like a live thing.

Now grasp the rod with the second and third fingers, and little finger of the left hand, leaving the thumb and first finger free to guide the line on the reel as you wind it (Figs. 155 and 156). Place the butt of the rod against the body and wind the reel with the right hand using the thumb and first finger to so guide the line that it will wind easily and spread over the whole spool, or hold it as in Figure 157, and use the thumb only to guide the line.

When fishing for real fish, black bass in particular, one uses the bait best adapted to the water in which one fishes. Crawfish, called crabs by country boys, are good bait in waters where the crawfish (crayfish) themselves live, crickets, minnows, hellgramites, which are also known as dobsons, bogarts and alligators, are loved by bass, but in casting we do not need to impale live creatures on the hook, we can use the artificial lures which makes much cleaner and more sportsmanlike work; one must be very careful, however, in handling lures with gangs of hooks. I speak feelingly as I had a man sink one of these hooks in my fingers and pull out a half inch of the nerve of the finger. Incidently I may mention that I was never dumped overboard, stuck with a hook or had any of the minor accidents, painful and unpleasant which may occur to one when hunting and fishing, except said accident was caused by some bungling tenderfoot, in other words, by some untrained person.

How to Fasten a Hook to a Line

If your hook is not attached to a snell take a piece of gut, tie a knot in it as in Figure 164, turn the loose end through the eye of the hook, then run the barb of the hook up through the loop (see dotted line, Fig. 164), pull the knot tight and you will have Figure 165. The knot you have just tied is a slip-knot and by pulling on the loose end of the gut you will shorten the loop until you have Figure 166. This is a better way than Figures 167 and 168, because in Figure 166 the strain on the gut does not come directly against the loop, as it does in Figures 167 and 168, many fishermen, however, do not take the trouble to do this but use the jam hitch shown in Figure 169. When this is tightened up it makes a good hitch.

How to Snell a Hook

In the first place the shanks of fish hook are unnecessarily long, so take a pair of pliers and snip off about one third of the shank. Boys generally have real home grown teeth and know how to use them, such tools come in handy in snelling a hook with fine tying silk, pink color preferred. Take one end of the silk with your teeth and hold the other end

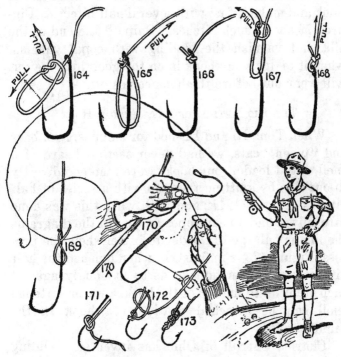

with your forefinger and thumb (Fig. 170). After waxing the tying thread with shoemaker's wax, make a loop at one end of a link of gut (as already described and depicted by Figures A, B, C, D, E, opposite Figure 115. Also 136–139). Scrape the other end with the sharp blade of your jack-knife until the gut is sharpened like a led pencil for one

half inch to the end (Fig. 170A). Place the sharpened end on the back of the shank of the hook, hold
the hook as in Figure 170 and bind the gut to the
shank by winding the thread evenly and tightly
around shank and gut. Wrap it to the bend in the
hook and make it fast with several half hitches. Figure 172 shows such hitches. Snip off the end of the
silk and varnish the binding with copal varnish,
when it is dry your hook is on for good and the gut
will wear out before the hook comes off.

The Kid Method of Attaching a Hook

When Tom, Hi and I fished for sunnies, rock bass
and "pizen" cats, we had never seen or heard of a
snell or gut leader, our hooks were fastened directly
to our line by knitting them on with a series of half
hitches (Figs. 171, 172 and 173), when this was done
carefully it had a neat appearance. In the diagrams
the line is enlarged in order to better show the process, Figure 173 is unfinished, when finished the half
hitches are drawn taut so as to fit snugly against
each other up to the top of the hook, a water softened
snell can be attached neatly to a hook in the
same manner.

Charles Carroll of Ohio has invented a sliding
bobber or cork for use in bait casting. The contrivance is an ingenious one that would be especially useful to boys and, under certain conditions, to
men also.

The Sliding Cork

Is made of two pieces of cork (Fig. 175), of con-

venient size, joined together with a goose quill running through their centre (Fig. 176), use hot
shoemakers wax for glue and slip the quill (Fig. 174),
through the holes (Fig. 175) in the cork (Fig. 176).
Secure a glass bead that will slide easily through
the shank of the quill but not through the small end
of the quill (Fig. 174), push the bead in place and cut
off the quill to suit the cork (Figs. 176, 177 and 178),
the bead should now be on a level with the outside of

the cork. If you want
to make a real shop-
appearing cork, trim it
down to something ap-
proaching the conven-
tional form (Fig. 178),
sand paper it until it is
smooth when it may be
painted half red and
green or white.

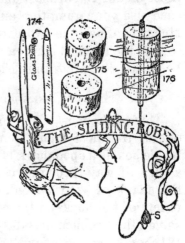

Tie a figure eight
knot (Fig. 179), in a
cotton string, and run
your fish line through
the loop as it is in Figure 170. This slipping knot
must be tight enough to hold under ordinary strain,
but fit easy enough on the line so that you can slide it
back and forth as the case may be with your fingers.
Now adjust the knot (K, Figs. 179 and 180) to agree
with the depth you want your bait to sink, fasten the
sinker (S, Fig. 177) to the leader, let it be heavy
enough to keep the float upright; slip the cork on the
line (Fig. 176), and make ready to cast, when the

bait hits the water it will sink until the bead at the top of the quill strikes the knot in the line and the bobber rides saucily on the surface.

Safety Pin Guides

It sometimes happens that one is so situated that it is not possible to secure the thimbles, rings or guides through which the line runs on a rod, and that those on our rod are lost, damaged or broken, in that case, use your gumption and twist bits of wire into rings then lash the two ends of the wire to the rod to hold the rings in place, a tip ring, for instance, can be made of a safety pin (Figs. 181 and 182).

Safety Corks for Gang Hooks

One of the most dangerous things to handle, and one of the most troublesome ones in one's fishing tackle box, is a spoonhook (Fig. 185), but if you make a cut half way through a cork through which to slip the shank of your spoonhooks, and then bury the points of the hooks in the cork (Fig. 185), you have solved the problem of safety first. Figures 183 and 184 show how to care for the grapple gang hooks when unattached to the spoon, the line is threaded through a hole made in the centre of the cork and then the line is drawn taut until the wicked barbs are rendered temporarily harmless by sheathing them in the cork.

The time I got one of those hooks under the tendons of my little finger, I was standing up in a boat. As soon as the tenderfoot saw what he had done, by disobeying orders, he made a grab at the hand to release my finger, but the consequence was

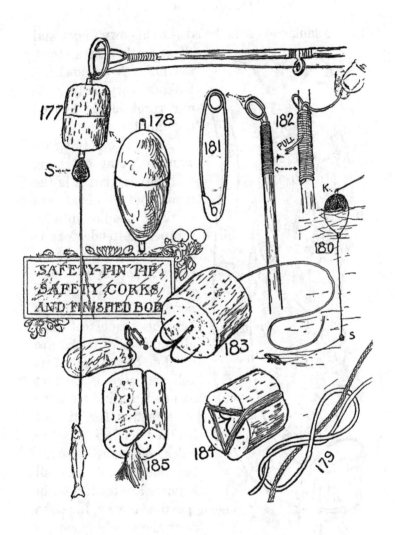

177

178

181

182 PULL

180

S

K.

S

SAFETY-PIN TIP
SAFETY CORKS
AND FINISHED BOB

183

185

184

179

that he sank one of the hooks into his own finger and there we two men stood, ten miles from nowhere, looking very silly with our right hands hooked together!

There is one thing we want to point out here, and that is, that it is the tenderfoot who is always getting people into a scrape. A tenderfoot is an inexperienced, untrained person and consequently a thoughtless person. Therefore, it is for the tenderfeet that all instructive books are written, because all of us fellows were tenderfeet at one time and we have an affection for all our brother tenderfeet. Besides, one must remember that all veterans, all experts are tenderfeet in some particular way, for none of us know the whole game, so when I said we write for tenderfeet that means that we write for everybody who is interested.

CORYDALUS HELLGRAMITE, BOGART, ALLIGATOR, HOJACK, DOBSON, OR CLIPPER

186

How to Keep Live Bait Alive

Boxes or pails for hellgramites* (Fig. 186), frogs, crawfish and other aquatic bait, are always cumber-

some and unhandy, besides, every time such receptacles are opened there is great danger of the bait escaping, especially if it be frogs, but I have found that an ordinary cotton sock (Fig. 187), when wet will keep such creatures alive, healthy and vigorous indefinitely, and at the same time one may thrust one's hand in the sock and secure a fresh bait without the slightest danger of the others escaping. Put your bait in the sock, then wet the sock thoroughly and slip the top of it

* The hellgramite is a harmless bluffer, and although it can pinch one's finger a little bit, no harm results; but it will be difficult to convince a novice of this fact at his first sight of this black, squirmy larvae. The young of the corydalis is about the most terrifying, vicious, repellent, creeping creature that we have among our American insects, and its popular names of flipflap, clipper, dobson, goggle goy, water grampus, Ho Jack, Hellgramite, conniption bug and hell devil fully testify to its ill appearance. The black bass, however, evidently thinks this hideous larvae is a delicious morsal. The diagrams, Figures 186 show the hellgramite and Figure 186A mamma corydalis with papa corydalis to the right, Figure 186C. It also shows the baby in its mummy state, Figure 186B, before it is transformed into a perfect insect.

through your belt and you are all ready for a days fishing.

We would love to go on and tell you all about the wily brook trout, the game qualities of the yellow perch, the fighting and sportsmanlike black bass, the fierce rushes of the pickerel, and all the devices deemed necessary for the capture of these fish, but we have given you the rudiments of fishing and, we hope, details enough to start you on your way to become famous anglers, for after all the only way to learn how to fish is to fish, and " if the Lord made fishing, a fellow oughter fish."

CHAPTER VI

JONATHAN CHAPMAN (JOHNNY APPLESEED)
OUR FIRST FORESTER ARBOR DAY
FORESTRY FOR YOUNG AND OLD

"What do we plant when we plant the tree?
We plant the house for you and me.
    We plant the rafters, the shingles, the floors,
    We plant the studding, the laths, the doors.
The beams and siding, all parts that be;
We plant the house when we plant the tree."

—Henry Abbey.

"ONCE upon a time, when dogs ate lime, and pea-cocks chewed tobacco," there was a stranger who visited the Ohio Valley. To be more accurate regarding the time, it was really in the year of 1749 that Céloron de Bienville hiked through the Ohio Valley loaded down with leaden plates. These were not dinner plates and all had inscriptions upon them. You must remember that this was back in the times when people had funny beliefs and that old Bienville had lodged in his "bean" the idea that by planting these lead plates in out of the way corners of the wilderness he was securing a legal title and a valid claim to this land for the old spendthrift and man about town, Louis XV of France, thus giving the King a title to land never purchased and which the King himself had never seen.

Now the interesting part of this incident lies in

the fact that nobody seemed to think that Bienville had "bats in his belfry," but everybody accepted him as a sane man. Nevertheless, fifty-two years later, when a real up-to-date forester by the name of Jonathan Chapman wandered through the forests with a pack horse bearing a burden of bags of apple seeds and proceeded to plant apple orchards in all the open glades, people significantly tapped their foreheads to indicate that the man was crazy!

JOHNNY APPLESEED

During the siege of Boston in the Revolutionary War, a little baby was born in that city, a baby boy, and his mother's thoughts were the good fairies who whispered in the baby's ears and moulded his character. The fairies danced around the cradle and the baby grew up to be a husky, clean young man, a scholar and a theologian.

Jonathan Chapman was a rather small but wiry young man, and when he did not give the better part of his clothes away, he was dressed in the costume of the day; but usually his charity left him but scantily attired. His lank black hair was not gathered after the manner of the day in a queue at his back, but it hung loosely down on his small but sturdy shoulders. His brow was high, and although his expression was as mild and winning as a woman's, his alert black eyes flashed beneath his calm brows with gleams of fire telling of the indomitable will and restless spirit of the real Pioneer and vigorous Scout, which his calm composure could not conceal. Johnny Appleseed wore a soft slight

mustache and scant beard in open rebellion against
the fashion of clean shaved faces which even the
woodsmen of that date (1801) were wont to follow.
He was unconventional in mind and manner, but no

one ever mistook him for aught but a real gentleman
and scholar.

Like Joan of Arc, he held intercourse with spirits,
and like the Quakers he consulted the "inner light,"
and being a disciple of Emanuel Swedenborg he
believed that he was surrounded by spirits—and who
can say he was not? And these spirits were none

other than the Good Turn Angels who were talking
to him, until at last he left the beaten tracks of men
and made his appearance in the wilderness of the
Ohio River Valley. Even there the Good Turn
Angels followed and told this youth that the wilderness was soon to be settled by white people, and that
it was his duty to enter the forests, follow the Indian
"traces" and the big game trails and prepare the
land for the reception of coming settlers.

Being inspired by Good Turn Angels, this Good
Turn Scout of the border declined to kill or injure
any living thing—plant, animal, bird, or insect.
He traveled unarmed and no creature molested
Jonathan Chapman, or "Appleseed Johnny" as he
patiently tramped over the trails with his loads of
appleseeds and the insane (?) idea of being of service
to mankind by starting nurseries of young trees and
planting orchards in every open glade he found.

The wild redmen knew him, and when they saw
him they held their fists up before their foreheads,
twisting them (the sign of mystery), then pointed to
heaven indicating that this white man's brain was
touched by the Great Mystery. The outlaws and the
desperados who fled to the wilderness to escape being
punished for their crimes always had a buffalo robe
and a place at their fireside for Appleseed Johnny
because he ministered to their sick, rendered first aid
to their wounded, and did his good turn without ask-
ing who or what his patients were.

Appleseed Johnny, or Johnny Appleseed, tra-
versed the wilderness from Pittsburgh to Indiana

and Illinois. He brought down, in dug-out canoes, bags of appleseeds, or sometimes he led a horse loaded with bags of appleseeds with which to start his nurseries, or even packed them on his own back. He secured the seeds at the cider presses at Fort Pitt and the settlements surrounding it, now the great smoky city of Pittsburgh.

When the tide riff, the first scum of emigrants, began to flow into the wilderness, following the trails that Chapman trod, they met and knew the Good Turn Scout, and like the redmen they also put their hands to their foreheads; but they did not make the redman's sign—they tapped their foreheads, indicating that Chapman's mind must be deranged, for they reasoned; how could a sane man with a warm coat deliberately take it off and give it to an emigrant who had none? Or take off his shoes and go barefooted over the frozen ground because some emigrant had no shoes? Or why should a sane man crawl out of a hollow log after he had sought shelter there, and all because he did not want to disturb two cub bears sleeping in the log? Rather than to wake up these forest babies our Good Turn Scout made his bed alongside of the log.

Now I ask you why did not the mother bear disturb the sleeping man when she came back to visit her babies? To the mind of the plodding emigrant this man must be crazy, for how could a sane man be so unselfish?

But if Johnny Appleseed was demented he was afflicted with the same sort of madness as was the

SLIPPERY ELM Ulmus fulva

great Founder of Christianity. Somehow or other the good fairies told the mother bear that Chapman was her friend; the sign of friendliness must have been stamped upon his face, and that is why the little children of the emigrants did not fear the gaunt, half-clad young man when they met him, but on the contrary would run laughing and smiling to meet him, would hang to such fragments of clothes as his generosity to others had left him. The children knew he was a Good Turn Scout, and they loved him.

Jonathan Chapman lived to be an old, old man, loved and revered by all who knew him. He led a life of usefulness, no one was too humble, no one was too great, no one was too good, and no one too bad for him to help. There are apple trees still flourishing which were planted in Indiana and Ohio by his hand, and in the springtime when the apple trees are all white with sweet scented blooms, and the soft winds scatter the petals of the flowers until they drift like snow through the air, these things are not ordinary flower petals they are the visible dreams and the thoughts of Johnny Appleseed, still showering the earth with his blessings.

ORIGIN OF ARBOR DAY

The people of Texas may celebrate Arbor Day on Washington's birthday; on the second of March they can celebrate the birthday of Texas' independence, and honor Davy Crockett, Colonel Bowie, Sam Houston, Deaf Smith and all the others of that band of heroes and empire makers of their great State.

Arbor Day is a legal holiday in Arizona, Maine, Maryland, New Mexico, Wisconsin and Wyoming, the day being set by the Governor; in Texas, February 22; Nebraska, April 22; Utah, April 15; Rhode Island, the second Friday in May; Montana, the second Tuesday in May; Georgia, the first Friday in December; Colorado (school holiday only) third Friday in April; Oklahoma, the Friday following the second Monday in March; Arkansas, the first Friday in March.

To the former Secretary of Agriculture, the Honorable J. Sterling Morton, belongs the honor of inventing Arbor Day, and the boys should all give Morton a rousing cheer on tree-planting day. Nebraska was the first to act upon his suggestion; next came the city of Cincinnati, then the States above named, and now Great Britain, France, Spain, New Zealand, and Japan all have an Arbor Day and all are following the example of our unique hero, Johnny Appleseed.

Every man and boy should be more or less a Johnny Appleseed, and especially should this be true of Boy Scouts. For over forty years their Chief Commissioner has been teaching the boys construction in place of destruction, teaching how to make in place of how to break, and that is the true scout idea. So let us get together and celebrate by planting some real trees which will grow in place of planting leaden plates that will not grow. Neither must we waste time and breath bewailing the mistakes of yesterday, but remember that to-day is ours in which to repair

the damage done by the prodigal sons of yesterday
and to save and protect what is left of our wonderful trees.

"Give fools their gold, and knaves their power,
    Let fortune's bubbles rise and fall;
Who sows a field, or trains a flower,
    OR PLANTS A TREE, IS MORE THAN ALL."
                        —John Greenleaf Whittier.

Sitting in my studio, under the head of a woodland caribou from far Alaska, facing the head of a
great, black moose from the forests on the border
line of Ontario, I have been wondering how a boy,
or a man, can really live in a treeless land. My
earliest recollection of a good time is that of picnics,
hikes, and excursions through the woods.

When our archæologists hunt for ancient civilization and dig to find the mummified remains of King
Tut and other fellows who lived thousands of years
ago but are now jerked meat, these antiquarians do
not go to fertile countries, but to places mostly waterless and uninhabitable; all provisions and water
supply must be carried to them. Now then, did it
ever occur to you that these ancient fellows who
owned powerful armies and built great cities, who
had art galleries, painting and sculpture, who had
baths and fountains, and all that sort of thing, could
not have had all these luxuries in the desert? In
other words, their civilization disappeared not so
much on account of wars and conquering nations, as
because they had used up the country in which they
lived, the fertile spots, the gardenlands and agricul-

ture lands had been deforested, like the old parts of China, and afterwards swallowed up by the deserts and the drifting sand thereof. Man might be defined as the desert making animal, and apparently he did not change his habits when he emigrated to America. On the contrary he set his wonderful brain to

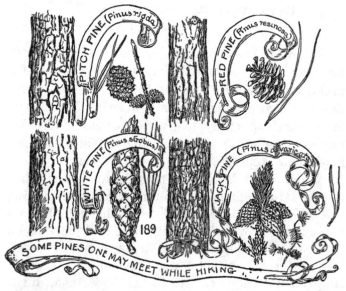

work to plan ways and means of spoiling what God had built and his brain has been busy ever since devising methods of destruction, methods of deforesting the lands, methods of draining the swamps which are the natural and only breeding grounds of our aquatic fowls, methods of destroying all live things, useful and otherwise, including men.

You young fellows who have your lives yet to live, you men of tomorrow, what sort of a land are you going to have after we men of yesterday have destroyed the forests, destroyed the animal life, even exterminated our beautiful wildflower, leaving you a country of squeaking European starlings, imported German carp, English sparrows, brown tail moths and boll weevils?

But cheer up! New York and New Jersey Scouts alone planted 141,000 trees in 1922 and 1923, which is encouraging and may be an object lesson to thoughtless people, for between our scientists who are inventing almost unbelievable methods of destruction and our ignorant people who do not realize and understand that our water supply and our very life is depending upon forests and the wild life of the country, there is a breach into which you young men and boys must leap and wave your banner of conservation, common sense, and usefulness. So "let's get busy right now" and set out some trees to celebrate Arbor Day, instead of sitting in school and singing some sentimental rhymes about them. Nursery rhymes may be all right to help children's minds grow, but they will not make trees grow.

After peace was declared the author, as National Scout Commissioner, tendered the services of the Boy Scouts of America to secure seeds of all sorts of trees with which France might reforest the devastated regions. This seemed to please the French officials mightily. Accompanied by Mr. John Burnham of the Camp Fire Club of America, the author visited the French Legation at Washington, and was received most graciously. But governments and government officials move slowly, and it was not

until months and months after this, and long after
the time when everybody was enthusiastic and keyed
up to concert pitch, that the author received word
from the French officials that they desired to inter-
view him; but he could then only say that the psychological moment had passed and it was too late.
Had they said "yes" when the author and Mr.

Burnham visited Wash-
ington, it is not too much
to say that not only every
Boy Scout in the United
States but almost every
boy who had the opportu-
nity to hike to the country
would have been hunting
seeds to send to France.
I am glad to say, however,
that on March 7, 1919, the
American Forestry Asso-
ciation furnished France
with enough Douglas fir
tree (Fig. 188) seeds to grow fifty thousand trees,
and so our scout work was not without fruit, as it
started the ball rolling!

The Planting of Forests

There are millions of acres of waste lands in the
United States which might be turned into forests
by boys' organizations within whose limits they lie.
On much of this land fine trees have grown and can
grow again.

Such a forest will be not only a productive investment, but involves no risk, and costs almost nothing to maintain. It demands next to no care. The ever increasing scarcity of timber makes a forest one of the safest and best investments a scout council or a school could make. Nothing is more certain of increasing steadily in value and finding a ready market at any time when it has to be converted into cash and in the meantime the land can be used as a recreation camp.

Even a small tract of woodland may prove a veritable gold mine. White pine (Fig. 189) is the ideal tree for forests in Pennsylvania and north of it, and from Minnesota eastward to the Atlantic seaboard. It is the best tree for general purposes of all-around usefulness. To reach very productive size it requires from thirty-five to seventy years, but at the end of that period a forest of white pine is worth $1,300 an acre. When only ten inches in diameter the trees are worth $2.50 apiece, and may be cut at a profit.

Walnut, beech and hickory nuts grow well in the Ohio Valley. The best kind of tree for town forests in California is the eucalyptus. It is a very rapid grower and furnishes fuel wood in a short time. For the Middle West, oak may be most desirable in one place and ash in another. In the plains region, of course, the trees selected must be able to stand long dry seasons.

The Catalpa speciosa (Western catalpa or cigar tree) is valuable. The Pennsylvania Railroad has made large plantings of Catalpa speciosa, intending to use the wood for railroad ties. Catalpa is very durable; the St. Louis Exposition exhibited some catalpa railway ties which were sound after thirty-five years use. A fencepost was exhibited which had given eighty years of service. Farmers are learning that the Catalpa speciosa ("hardy catalpa," Fig. 190, Fruit and Flower) is not a crooked-growing, worthless tree. Although the "southern catalpa" (catapla bignonoides) is usually unshapely.

If you are digging your own trees to transplant, do not allow the roots, even the smallest fibres, to become dry but roll them up in a ball of wet mud, or swamp moss (sphagnum) (Fig. 191); bind it with a piece of string, or use the rootlets of a tamarack or the bark of a dead chestnut, or any of the thousand and one things that one can find in the woods to use as string. If your trees come from the nursery, they should come with the roots done up in burlap, as in Figure 192.

In setting the trees, have a wash tub half full of thin mud. Dip the roots of each tree in this just before setting. Then place firmly in the hole (Fig. 193), making sure the trunk is perpendicular. Throw in over the roots some fresh surface dirt, *but never put in fresh manure*—it will kill them. Set the tree

an inch deeper than it stood in the nursery; the loose
dirt will settle and some of it may wash away. The
dirt should be pressed down firmly, forcing all the air
out and helping to retain the moisture. For some
trees plenty of water is necessary and in very dry

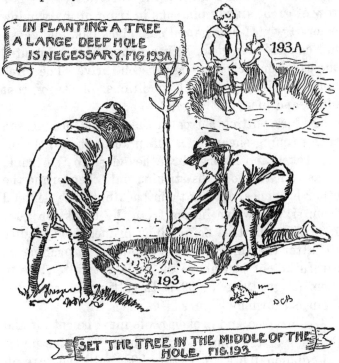

IN PLANTING A TREE
A LARGE DEEP HOLE
IS NECESSARY. FIG 193A

193A

SET THE TREE IN THE MIDDLE OF THE
HOLE FIG.193

earth water is necessary for almost any sort of tree.
Figure 194, watering the tree; Figure 195, trench of
earth made to hold the water until it soaks in.

There is a general impression that oaks are difficult to transplant, but they require only very careful handling. If the oak is moved once within five

years after the first transplanting, so as to get new and abundant fibre, and is carefully planted in rich soil it will grow. But a tree from four to eight feet high must be used, not a large dumpy tree. The pin oak is one of the best growing varieties (there is a row of great sturdy pin oaks in front of my window where I write) but the red oak, black oak, and chestnut oak are also good. When properly transplanted the ash, horse-chestnut and beech thrive. The birch must be given good soil conditions, plenty of root fibres and plenty of water.

Before putting a tree in the ground one person with pruning shears or a sharp knife should cut off all broken and injured branches close to the trunk, so as to leave no stubs sticking out; then prune the other branches, cutting them back until they extend from six to twelve inches from the trunk. Figure 196 shows the tree before it is pruned, and Figure 197 after the knife has been applied. In pruning be careful to cut just above the buds but quite close to them (Figs. 198 and 199). In cutting the roots cut them as shown by Figure 200.

All bruised and broken roots must be cut off and the ends of the long roots cut back from the under side diagonally, as in Figure 200, until they are all one length, making the root the size to fit in the hole which is to receive it. Arrange the tree so that the side having the most branches faces the south, the way it grew in its original bed. The "Chief Forester" should provide himself with a piece of string with a small stone tied to the end of it, to use as a

plumb-bob and by its means set the tree perpendicular (Fig. 201). Put some rich top-soil in the bottom
of the hole, tramp it down firmly, then spread some
fine top-soil over it. Set the roots of the tree in the
hole; while one person holds the tree in place with
one hand, he can use the other to straighten out and

arrange the rootlets, and the first fellow can shovel
in more top dirt, a little at a time. While one shovels
the other works the dirt in with his fingers among the
roots. When the hole is half-filled, the dirt may be
carefully tramped down around the trunk, the rest of
the soil shoveled in, and the trick is done.

To put trees in a straight line erect a rod at one
end of the proposed line and put a peg at the other
end (Fig. 201), then take your plumb-line, shut one
eye and squint along the string to the rod, while
another fellow holds a pole up and moves it to the
right or left according to directions until it is in line

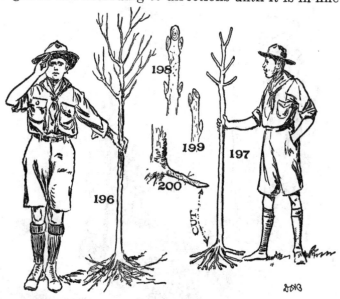

between the plumb-line and the rod; then he marks
the place and drives a peg (Fig. 201). Of course,
when you plant a tree you must remove the peg, but
you will not lose the place if you use a

PLANTING BOARD

four feet long by four inches wide with a notch in
the centre and a notch at each end (Fig. 202). Before
digging the hole for the tree place the board down

on the ground so that the centre notch fits against
the peg, then drive two pegs, one at each end notch.
Now you see you can take up your board, pull up
the line peg, and dig the hole. After the hole is dug
put the board back again and set your tree to fit the
middle notch, which is exactly where the line peg
stood; it will then be in line with all the other trees
(Fig. 203).

PRUNING TREES

You must not expect a workman, even though he
be directed by park officials, to trim a limb off a tree
properly; they simply won't do it, because it is too
much trouble. Therefore, you will have to do it your-
selves. If you cut a large limb off as shown in Figure
204, when the weight of the limb causes it to fall it
will tear the bark off down the tree trunk, and even if
it should not the stub would cause decay. Figure
205 shows such a branch a year after cutting. Figure
206 shows it five years after, Figure 207 shows it ten
years old, Figure 208 shows a section of the trunk
with the dead tooth in the gum, so to speak. Figure
209 shows where the dead branch started to decay
in the trunk. Figure 210 shows the usual way a cut
is made by those who know better but are too lazy to
do it right. Figure 211 shows the proper way—three
cuts to remove a large limb. The first is an undercut
about half the way through, the second is an upper-
cut about half the way through; the weight of the
branch will cause it to break off with the fracture
connecting these two cuts, leaving a stub. The stub
must be sawed off close to the trunk, as shown by the

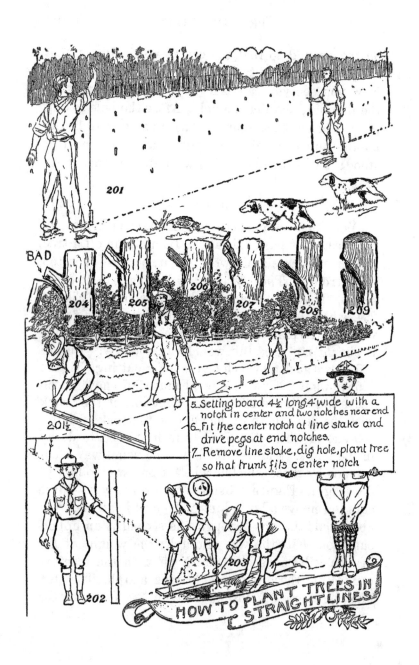

201

BAD

204 205 206 207 208 209

201½

5. Setting board 4½' long 4" wide with a notch in center and two notches near end
6. Fit the center notch at line stake and drive pegs at end notches.
7. Remove line stake, dig hole, plant tree so that trunk fits center notch

202

203

HOW TO PLANT TREES IN STRAIGHT LINES.

third cut in Figure 211. This will leave an up-and-down wound. A wound exposing the wood is healed by the growth of the cambium (Fig. 212) which gradually forms new tissue covering the scar (Fig. 213) until it is completely healed (Fig. 214). The exposed wood of the wound should be daubed with coal tar to protect it from moisture and decay.

Figure 212 shows the section of a one year old sapling; Figure 215 is a fire-wounded tree, neglected and allowed to rot, making a hollow. Nature does her best to heal this wound, but the inner and outer bark, while trying, find no bearing on which the growing bark can rest, so it curls in on itself (Fig. 216) in the hollow trunk. Figures 217 and 218 are methods of straightening trees. Figure 219 is a makeshift tree box to protect the tree from livestock.

If one of my readers discovers a pair of the Canada ducks breeding, many scientific "guys," with high brows and hearts of dust, would pay him almost any sum for the skins and eggs of those poor birds, because their skins and eggs are exceedingly *rare,* and thus drive the reader into the crime of wiping out the species altogether. Therefore it is up to you, boys, Scouts, and young men, to put some warm blood in the scientist's dusty heart, to put some warm blood in the lumberman's avaricious heart, and to put some warm blood in the commercial hearts of all our people. You can best start this crusade by making a great day of Arbor Day and planting thousands and thousands of trees, and making a wilderness saint of old Johnny Appleseed.

It was the author who first made the suggestion that memorial trees be planted for those of our soldiers who made the supreme sacrifice. In the "American Boy." of March, 1919 he said:

"In the service flags of every community throughout our country there shine many golden stars. The

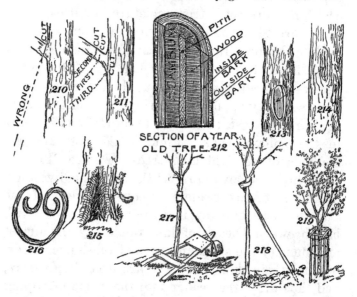

service flags in time will be worn out, the cloth will disintegrate and fall apart, and as a matter of record the flag itself will disappear.

"But we want those golden stars to be imperishable, we want them to last forever as an inspiration to coming generations, and they will last if we work up a proper sentiment. Now then, if each community will plant a tree for each golden star and put a tablet with the name of the hero it stands for on that tree, we will have a living monument for every one of our boys who died 'Over There' and we can believe without much stretch of our imagination that the souls of our soldier boys will enter those trees and cause them to grow and thrive, and the soldier boys' names will live with the trees as does that of Jonathan Chapman in the Ohio Valley. Be this true or not, we know that our 'gold star trees' are really blessing our land.''

CHAPTER VII

HOW TO STALK, TO PHOTOGRAPH THEM OR EVEN TO CAPTURE WILD ANIMALS WITH YOUR NAKED HANDS

MANY, many years ago, maybe it was about the year 1776—and maybe it wasn't—at any rate, it was when the author was too small to be a scout, but not too small to be a naturalist, he loved all sorts of wild things, and although his daddy was a celebrated shot and his brothers were all hunters, the author did not like to kill things, but he would have been delighted to fill his backyard with every live creature the forests contained, including even wolves, bears and panthers.

The little fellow was firmly convinced that he could handle all these wild creatures if he could once get "next to them." That conviction has been rudely shaken several times since those happy days and, when an innocent looking bear with an angelic expression ruined his uniform last fall by ripping it with its sharp claws it still further unsettled his belief and confidence in his ability to gentle all sorts of wild creatures hurriedly. As a small boy, however, he did not meet any sort of wild animals larger than a fox, and with handling the smaller mammals he had very good success; but that is another story.

The author had no money with which to buy animals, and if he had had money there were no stores, as there are now, where one may purchase all sorts of queer live things. Consequently if he wanted a menagerie in his back yard he must secure the animals himself; but how?

For hours the little fellow might have been seen stretched out on the lawn, his chin on his dirty hands watching a cat stalking birds. The boy noted that the cats were very successful. They could catch the wildest birds, birds that a human being could not approach without causing instant flight, so he studied the cat's actions to learn its methods, and then he made the same discovery that the wild men of the world had made thousands and thousands of years ago, and that the cat had discovered even before men had learned the trick.

The boy noted that the old cat stalking a robin on the lawn crouches down and keeps still until the robin is off its guard and then quickly and silently advances until the alert bird's suspicions are aroused, when again the cat "freezes," that is, becomes motionless. The cat does not make a false move. The cat does not go romping after the bird: it makes no leap until it is within striking distance, and it has the patience of Job. It advances only when the prey is not watching. All things being equal the bird is bound to die.

But in these cases all things were not equal, because a boy with a scout's heart was there, a boy who wanted to learn how to stalk and also the reason for the success of the feline hunter; but the boy loved not to kill, he loved the birds, and just before the cat could make a spring he would sail his hat at the bird and frighten it away. After a while he thought he would try the cat's tactics himself. A couple of wild pigeons—passenger pigeons (Fig. 220), such as no longer exist on earth, visited the barnyard; beautiful old-rose colored birds with long tails, clean cut bodies and bright eyes, necks scintillating with metallic reflections . . . Oh, they were wonderful birds! But they are all in the Happy Hunting Ground now! Well, these birds were indiscreet enough to alight not far from the barn where they were busily picking up chicken feed, a very unusual thing to do. The boy had seen wild pigeons feeding in the beech trees, but of the millions of wild pigeons observed at various times these were the only two he can remember seeing feeding on the grounds in a barnyard.

Here was a glorious opportunity to try the tactics of the cat. The pigeons were at a great disadvantage because they must fly towards the boy to get by him. They could not fly the other way without dashing against the side of the barn. The boy took this in at a glance. As he crept up on the feeding birds they became nervous, stretched their necks and seemed to be ready to fly; but then the lad would freeze, stand immovable, and gradually the birds would again become interested in the chicken feed. My, that was a glorious hunt; no big game hunts that the author has since indulged in can compare with the thrills that he felt on that occasion! As if to help the boy in his purpose the pigeons when alarmed would walk towards each other, stretch their necks around, then go to pecking corn again, as if the society of each other gave them courage. How long it took to stalk those two beautiful birds I do not know—it may have been hours. The boy felt as if he could have kept it up for a day, but at last the opportunity arrived and with arms extended he dashed for the pigeons. He hardly expected to be successful, but did hope that he could catch one of the birds. Imagine his joy when the two birds flew right at his head and he grabbed one fluttering bird in each hand!

He could not believe that it had really happened, but he had reasoned all along that if a cat could catch birds he could, for he at least *had as much sense as a cat!* He was prouder of proving his intellectual equality with Tabby than he has ever been since in any intellectual victory at school or with men. Now that he had the pigeons he had no place to put them. You see the charm of this sort of hunting is that one does not know what one is about to catch. He did not go out for pigeons; their advent was an accident. One thing was evident the boy could not forever hold those birds; so he inserted the pigeons in the dog-house, put a board at the opening and later made a real door of slats for the kennel. The birds took very kindly to confinement and later when they by chance escaped they flew around a while and came back to the doghouse.

I was telling my good old friend, John Burroughs, about these things, and he was intensely interested. He did not see how it was possible for a man to go out and catch a wild bird with the bare hands, until I explained to the great naturalist that probably it

SAFETY FIRST
GRIP

was not possible for a man to avow that he is going to catch a bird, start out for that purpose and bring back a live bird. You see, Mr. Burroughs made the same mistake that is in your mind now, of supposing that I would go out anywhere and catch a bird, but that is not possible or true. What I did do was to catch a bird when the *opportunity offered*. My boyish study of natural history and the habits of animals had taught me to recognize the opportunity when I saw it, and the cat had taught me how to take advantage of it.

I was going to say that  any of you boys can do this, but I must modify that and say that any boy with a natural aptitude for this sort of thing can learn to do it, just the same as a boy with a talent for drawing can learn to be an artist, one with an ear for music can learn to be a musician, so one with a feeling for wild creatures, a sympathy for their wants and thoughts can learn to stalk and catch them by hand. To do this, you must know what the bird is thinking about

 when it begins to get restless, otherwise it will take you by surprise and you will miss it. I have caught sparrows, robins, thrushes, wild pigeons, quail, ruffed grouse, a crow and all but caught an owl. I mean the big Virginia owl; I have caught many of the little screech owls. Now the reason I did not catch that big Virginia owl was because he had a couple of big catchers himself, with long hooked talons on them

like those of an eagle; so when I slipped up on him and looked him over, I simply said "good night, boo-boo." and I struck him with the palm of my hand, knocking him off his perch, and away he flew. Afterwards I caught one of the same sort of owls (Fig. 221) but that was easy, for the owl had struck a telegraph wire which felled it to earth. A rolling-mill hand came along and made the mistake of putting his cowhide clad foot on the owl. When I came up the man's blood was oozing out of his rough shoe. The owl was on its back, clawing up in the air and snapping its beak. Now here is where I saw my opportunity. The bird was not clawing sideways, this way and that, but straight up and down, so kneel-down beside him I quickly slid my arm between his legs, grasped him by the throat, lifted him up and held him as one would hold a game cock with one leg on each side of my arm, the same as the fox is held in Figure 224, Figure 223 is the owl which shouts "Hoo-hoo! Hoo-hoo! Hoo-ah!"

There was no danger in doing this—the rolling-mill man got hurt because he did not know an opportunity when he saw it, but the owl did!

One can catch small, and even comparatively large mammals the same way. I once picked up a red fox (Fig. 224) that the dogs had driven into a farm house where he had fled under the bed, and was lying with his back against the wall in the corner, with his mouth open. The fox was frightened almost to death and I picked it up exactly as I picked up the big owl, took him home with me, put a collar on his neck and kept him, although I must say that he never

SAFELY WATCHED

MUSKRAT

225

VERY DANGEROUS

Grasping Claw of an
Eagle

226

FIERCE IN APPEARANCE BUT
NOT VERY DANGEROUS

DANGEROUS, WILL
PUT OUT YOUR EYES

227

CAN BITE
VICIOUSLY

224

HELD THUS
HE IS HELPLESS

Dangerous Weapons.

became a very affectionate or trustworthy pet. Now
I would not advise any boy to try to catch a red
fox, a 'coon (Fig. 222) or even a muskrat (Fig. 225)
until he learns the habits of these animals very
thoroughly. The 'coon can put up a very nasty fight,
the muskrat can bite off your finger, and even a
'possum can bite you severely. Yet I have caught all

these animals without being hurt, and all with my
bare hands; but mind you I will not promise to do
it again! I will say, however, that if I see a chance
where it can be done successfully I will not hesitate
to try it. All of which means that to be a stalker one
must be a thorough nature student; not a book
naturalist—it won't help you to catch birds in the
least if you know the Latin name of every bird in the
United States, neither will it prevent you from being
terribly cut up with the talons of a bird of prey

(Fig. 226) or being stabbed by a heron's beak (Fig.
227) or hurt by a crow (Fig. 228) because you know
all about the bird's family name, the names of his
cousins and his aunts, where he ranges and where he
nests, as the books tell you. But what you must know
is what that bird is thinking about; just what it can
and will do in certain emergencies.

I said that I would not promise to go out and
catch a bird, but once I did make such a promise. I
noticed that a one-eyed crow frequented a certain
brush heap where it hunted mice. Now Mrs. Beard
did not believe much in the ability of anyone to
catch wild creatures, and when I told her that I was
going out and catch the crow she laughed immoder-
ately and said that the man doesn't live who can
catch a crow. I protested that this crow had but
one eye, to which she replied:

"My dear, I grew up on a farm. I've known
crows all my life, and you couldn't catch a crow if it
was blind in both eyes."

Well, an hour afterwards there was a terrible
squawking and I brought the one-eyed crow into the
cabin and tossed it down on the floor in front of her.
She looked at the crow in dismay and she looked at
me; then with that wonderful logic which belongs to
the sex, she said:

"Open the door and let that horrid thing out.
I don't believe you caught it even now!"

The boy who is a past master in the art of stalking need never complain of the lack of game, he need
never be loaded down with heavy arms and amuni-
tion. But stalking, as you may understand from the

foregoing, does not mean lying in wait all night at some spring or waterhole, or slopping around in a cold, wet blind, camouflaged with cat tails, amidst a flock of wooden ducks, but it does mean infinite patience. Stalking was practiced by the American Indians, and by the American Pioneers. The Indian's arrows did not shoot as far as the modern high-power guns—he had to be close to his game before he could hit it. Even a crack shot like George Washington had to be within fifty yards of the buck before he felt that he could be certain to hit it. But to stalk a deer or any of the larger game animals you must keep to the windward of it. All these creatures have wonderful noses and the one scent they dread most is the scent of man—a taint of man on the breeze will stampede a herd of wild animals. I've known it to stampede grizzly bear, so you see that there is a lot to learn in this stalking business. The stalker must go with eyes open, ears open, and nostrils open, ready at a moment's notice to turn himself into a stump, that is, to freeze at the sight of game, then to run silently, stooping low in the shadow of a cliff or bank, and dodging like a coyote. Personally, I have never been able to stalk a coyote—whenever I have tried it the animal always kept out of gunshot ahead of me, ever and anon sitting on a rise of the ground, where with its body silhouetted against the sky it would await my approach then dive down into the swail and be off again, until I discovered that I was not having fun with the coyote, the coyote was having fun with me.

The favorite way of hunting these prairie wolves

is by seating oneself on the edge of a waterhole or
a spring in the early morning, because coyotes have
a habit of stopping for a drink before retiring after
their night's hunting trip.

I once stalked a buck deer. It was raining, and
the kerosene cans I had on my arm struck together
and made a noise like a cowbell. The old buck lay so
quietly in the brush that I was not quite sure whether
it was a real deer or an imaginary one; but when I
was within fifteen feet of him he shot up in the air
is if he had been in a spring trap. I don't know
which was the most startled, the deer or the author.
I sat right down in the mud. The deer stood a frac-
tion of a moment looking at me, then his body
dropped, his legs bent and he stole away like a
shadow. The whole thing was so quick and sudden
that it was necessary for me to put my hand on the
deer bed and feel that it was still warm before I
could convince myself that I had really stalked the
old buck.

But if you want to prove yourself to be a real,
genuine stalker, try your skill on stalking a bob-cat
or a Canadian lynx—then you are up against a
stalker that can outstalk you. Once when I was trout
fishing, a lynx seated himself in the road near the
brook. I picked up a stone and ran towards him,
but he sat quietly in the road looking at me. As I
approached him I slackened my pace. When I got
real close, that is, as close as I wanted to be, I made
up my mind that it would be mean to throw stones
at a poor old lynx, so I went to the brook, picked up
my rod, and continued fishing. The truth was I had

lost no wild-cat, and besides their fur is no good in trout fishing time.

Every one who wants to stalk live creatures must learn the habits of the creatures, and there is no better way to learn their habits than by trying to stalk them. By careful work one may get close enough to a deer or even a moose, not only to hit it with a stone but I might almost say to hit it with one's hat. The first thing you must fix in your mind is to Stop, Look and Listen. Move slowly and silently, stopping every little while, and fix your mind on what you are doing and nothing else. Remember that for the time being you are a hunting animal, with your heart and soul and all your faculties intent upon your pursuit. Make careful note of everything that happens—I do not mean to take out a pencil and write it down, but note it in your mind. If a twig snaps turn your head very slowly in the direction from which the sound came. Teach yourself to detect the different odors of the woods and name them. In a short time you will be able to detect the odors of live creatures when they are near you, to detect the odor of a forest fire before anyone else suspects its existence, to smell the pine and all the sweet scents of the wilderness and know what they mean.

Stalking will test your power of eyesight, your keenness of observation, the sharpness of your hearing and the delicacy of your olfactory nerves—which in plain language means your ability to smell things. If you do not know in what direction you must walk to find the animals for which you are searching, then wet your finger and hold it aloft. Do this frequently;

the cold side of your finger will tell you the direction from which the wind comes. Never put yourself in such a position that the wind will blow from you towards your quarry, because wild animals, almost without exception, depend upon their noses to detect the presence of an enemy. Remember, some game, the moose in particular, will double upon its track, and if you are following a bull moose trail you may walk right by him where he is lying in the shrubbery watching you. Also remember that it is extremely improbable that any wild animal will charge you or attack you in the open. The bear that tore the writer's clothes did so because he mistook the intent of a move the man made to retrieve a piece of candy from the ground. The bear thought the man meant fight, so struck him with both claws, not because he was looking for a fight, but to defend himself. He was a Yellowstone Park bear and had learned not to place too much confidence in the funny two-legged animals which frequent that park by the thousands every year, many of whom never before saw a loose bear. The writer has seen men go up and kick at the bears in the Park, and take big sticks and chase them, all of which does not inspire Bruin with much confidence in our race, or create any real love for us. But while this cinnamon bear attacked the man because he stooped down to pick up a piece of candy, the same man has more than once thrown grizzly bears into a panic by suddenly standing up from a crouching pose and shouting "Boo!" The grizzly bear, however, is too dangerous and powerful an

animal to try to fondle or pet. If, however, you give
him plenty of room to pass he as a rule will observe
the same courtesy to you.

CALLING

The American Indians made a point of being able
to imitate the calls of all the wild creatures in their
vicinity. They used those calls not only for the purpose of enticing the game to within the range of their
bows, but also used the calls as signals among themselves. They could imitate perfectly the howl of the
wolf, the scream of the panther, or the bleating of a
fawn. The Indians and the old backwoods scouts and
buckskin men of the border could call up the mother
deer by bleating like a fawn. The northern Indians
still grunt like the moose through megaphones made
of birchbark in order to bring game up to within
shooting distance of the tenderfeet they are paid
to guide.

It is claimed by old hunters that the moose calling
should be done in the morning along with the first
streak of dawn, or in the evening. One writer says:

"It will be noted that calling can be done only in
a dead calm, for the reason that if the slightest breeze
blows—a steady breeze anyhow—the bull will not
answer, but will circle your position, get your scent,
and then good-by Sir Moose. Bulls have all sorts
of ways of coming. As a general thing the very big
chaps and the youngsters are the wariest, and sometimes will approach and even appear without 'having
spoken' once."

My old friend, the late Andrew J. Stone, after

whom several of the northern big game animals are named, always declared that any old sound would bring up a bull moose in the rutting season, and gave instances where the sound of the ax had brought a bull moose from cover, and where the Indians had taken a stick and rattled it upon an old pair of antlers with the same result.

Once when the writer was in camp on the shore of a lake in northern Canada, there was, back of the woods where his tent was pitched, a small "moose lake"; while sitting around the camp fire at night we could hear the grunting of the moose over in the neighborhood of the lake. Sometime in the night the writer got his shoulder out of his sleeping bag. It was cold, raw weather with five or six inches of wet snow on the ground and the raw wind chilled the exposed shoulder and set the sleeper to sneezing. The sneezes were immediately answered by the grunt of a bull moose, and in a few minutes he could be heard crashing through the woods in the close proximity of the tent. With that the author experimented by sneezing again, and each time he sneezed he was answered by the grunt of the moose. At last he crawled out of his sleeping bag, took up his rifle, and went outside his tent, but the sky was overcast, the campfire had died down, and he could not see six feet in front of him. He stumbled around for a while and could hear the moose crashing around close by. The moose did not run away, but the hunter being in his stocking feet, felt the chill of the wet snow to be too uncomfortable, and retired to his tent,

where he had to feel around for a dry pair of socks
and then crawl back into his sleeping bag shivering
with the cold and blaming himself for being so foolish as to try to find a moose in the dark. But the
point of the incident is that the moose was called by
a sneeze, also on a pitchy dark night, notwithstand-
ing that some authorities claim one can have no success calling at night unless it be bright moonlight.

So many of these instances occur that one is
forced to believe that there is a lot of fiction in regard
to the necessity of making a good imitation of the
cow moose, or the bull, as the occasion may be. However, for art's sake and for woodcraft's sake, one
should practice the call until one can imitate
it perfectly.

The writer has on more than one occasion called
the Baltimore oriole down to within a few feet of
where he was standing by imitating the bird's own
call. He has often amused himself by calling to the
different singing birds and while it did not bring
them to him as did the call of the oriole, they would
almost invariably stop singing, cock their heads on
one side, listen intently, and then start on again
with their song. Sometimes, if the bird happened to
be a brown thrasher or a catbird, it would attempt
to imitate the whistle of the man and upon experi-
ment some of the birds unmistakably imitated a note
or two of a bugle call.

Since writing the preceding the author has
visited Wheeling, West Virginia, and had Wetzel's
Cave pointed out to him, a dark hole in the stony

bank. The interesting thing about this cave is that it is where the Indian hid when he gobbled like a wild turkey and thus lured the settlers out to their doom. One day the famous scout Wetzel was roaming the woods when he heard the familiar call of a wild turkey; but Wetzel was a wise woodsman. He knew that several white men had been scalped in that immediate vicinity, and good as was the imitation of the turkey call, it did not fool this long haired terrible Indian hater. Stooping down in the underbrush the "Night Wind" as he was called watched the mouth of the cave until the feathered head of an Indian appeared. The crack of Wetzel's rifle put a stop to the gobble of the turkey and a fresh scalp at Wetzel's belt told the reason why that gobbler was never afterward heard in the neighborhood of what is now known as Wetzel's Cave.

Every boy should learn the different calls of the birds in his neighborhood, and to distinguish between their cries of alarm and their social talk, because if the lad gives a cry of alarm he will stampede the birds in place of collecting them. Not only do the birds know each others' cries of alarm, but so also do the fur bearing mammals. I have seen the gray squirrels scurry and dive into their holes in the old dead trees instantly, when the watchful old crow detected the hated presence of man and called out a warning to the other crows.

Boys should also know how to croak like a frog, sing or whistle, or whatever their buzzing noise may be called, like a hoptoad, chirp like a peep-frog, chatter like a squirrel, hoot like an owl, as well as whoop like an Indian.

It is well known to detectives and woodsmen that nothing can exist on this earth without creating some sign, trails or marks which may be read by such as are educated for that purpose, that is, by those whose power of observation has been developed by study and practice, and whose ability to reason from cause to effect and from effect back to cause has also been developed by practice and study. Thus, a 'coon climbing a tree leaves the marks of its claws upon the trunk (we are speaking of a raccoon now, not a colored person) and if it climbs the tree frequently these marks will be quite noticeable to the 'coon hunter, 'though they might be passed by without thought by a college professor, by a Ph.D., an LL.D. or even a D.D., for college degrees do not necessarily develop the same brain muscles as does a life in the woods and the open.

Now then, the scratches on the tree trunk are the *effect;* the 'coon climbing the tree is the *cause.* If one comes to a tree with a trunk which is scratched in the manner described, one must reason back from effect (the marks) to the cause (the 'coon), after which even a chump will know that one is very likely to find a 'coon up that tree.

We make the illustration of the 'coon simply because that happened to come first in our mind, but the white-footed mouse, the vole or the short-tailed meadow rat, Molly cottontail or gray rabbit, Reynard the fox, Uncle Ephraim the grizzly bear, or any other animal or moving object is bound to leave its sign, its trail, its mark, unless said animal or object travels through the air or water.

Live creatures must eat and drink. They cannot drink without leaving tracks to the water and they cannot eat without leaving traces of their feast. If it is a mountain lion, a wolf, a catamount or a fox, there must necessarily be bones, blood, fur, feathers, or similar material left after the feast, and these things will attract a woodsman's attention, and if he is a good woodsman it will require little more than a glance to tell him exactly who among the forest folks feasted there.

If the creature is an herbivorous animal, that is, an animal which feeds on vegetables, it will be seen that the grass has been cropped, the branches nipped, the bark chewed, and the berries picked; and these facts will attract a woodsman's attention. If a stone falls off a bank and rolls down, it is bound to leave a trail or trace of some sort behind it. If a deer jumps off a bank and bounds away (Fig. 229), its dainty sharp hoofs will mark the place where the feet struck. The length of the stride or the space between the different hoof marks will tell the observer whether the animal was moving rapidly or slowly.

Now wait a moment! We want to make this thing plain. If the hoof marks are close together the animal cannot have been moving very rapidly. Is it not a fact that when you are in a hurry you stretch your legs? Well, so does a deer; so does a fox; so also does the big, lumbering moose; and thus when in a hurry they leave long spaces between their tracks.

From "Traces" to Railroads

Noting these things, and reasoning from them,

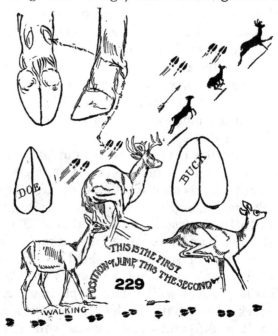

is what is meant by reading the trail or tracks. In the olden days the pioneers called these marks a trace; they followed the traces left by Indians, and these traces gradually became paths. Then the pack animals came along and the mules and horses with the packs on their backs following these paths transformed them into well defined trails. Then the lumbering, great, old-fashioned prairie schooner, or freight wagon, came along, and the rude trails were transformed into rough roads. Following the freight and moving with it came the settlers; towns and villages sprang up at the crossroads. Tolls were collected; taxes imposed and spent on improving the roads; and the roads were transformed into turnpikes, over which the old-fashioned stagecoach lumbered and jolted, or into railroads—and today most of the Indian traces are marked by the glistening steel rails of our great railroad system.

The railroad engineers were following the trail of the vanished redmen, and the redmen followed the trail of vanished big game. The elk, the buffalo, and the deer of the wilderness selected the easiest way over the mountain ridges, picked out the most practical fords on the rivers and thus made the first traces or trails on this continent.

THE VALUE OF WOODCRAFT

Now then, what is the value of woodcraft? Is it a fad? Is it just a game to play? Why bless your souls, this whole continent and the civilization thereof are built upon the early knowledge of woodcraft. Therefore when we tell you to go out in the woods and study woodcraft, we are not only telling you to do something that you will enjoy but we are telling you to do something that is every bit as practical as your grammar, your arithmetic, your Latin and your Greek.

The trouble with most specialists is that they cannot see beyond their specialties; sometimes college professors and school teachers think only in the line of their profession. Many a school teacher and college professor left in the woods would be like the little babes in the nursery book, the story that brings tears to the children's eyes.

> "And when they were dead
> The robins so red,
> Brought strawberry leaves
> And over them spread."

There is this difference between the education you get in the woods and the education you get in school. The education you get in the woods makes a better pupil of you at school, but nothing but book knowledge may make a fool of you in the woods. The real way for you to do is to combine the two and then you make a real man, a big man, a great man, like Audubon, Thoreau, John Burroughs, Lincoln or Washington.

WATCH FOR SIGNS

When paddling along silently in your canoe, if you come to a shallow place, in a northern wilderness lake, where all the grass that grows under the water has been disturbed and a lot of the plants uprooted and left floating on the surface, that is a sign! Be careful! Make no noise with your paddle, but peer over the sides of your canoe into the water and you will probably see the tracks of some big, cloven-footed animal, tracks like those made by a big ox. Yes, your heart will beat faster, for those are the tracks of our biggest game animal, the moose.

The water may be still muddy; that tells you that the game has been there quite recently. The moose feed upon the subaqueous plants (that is another valuable school-teacher word—sub means under, as you know from submarine, and subaqueous means under water) but since we are only woodsmen we will speak of them as under-water plants.

Sometimes one may find the roots of the yellow water lily (splatter dock) floating around, and the roots may have teeth marks on them; one glance will tell you, however, that the animal that bit those roots was a rat-like animal, a gnawer—what your teacher would call a rodent—and then you know that the king of forest handicrafters has been there, that the most shy of all woods people, the beaver, has been feeding there overnight.

Get out of your canoe, walk up through the yellow grass of a little meadow between the shores of the lake and the forest of balsams, cedar, and spruce, and follow the ravine or swale back into the wilderness until you come to the thickets of Labrador tea on the shores of a lake, and there it is possible you may discover that some large animal has been lying down, has made what we call a bed; that when the animal left its bed it nibbled the branches of the bushes as it walked, that is, it browsed on the bushes and the tracks it left were like those of domestic cattle.

At once you know that a moose has been taking a siesta, a daytime nap, and that it has awakened and walked leisurely away, that it was not in a hurry— if it had been in a hurry it would not have taken time to have nibbled off the tops of the bushes. You know that it is a bull moose, because you have found a large sized alder and discovered that the bark is rubbed off where the animal has been scratching its

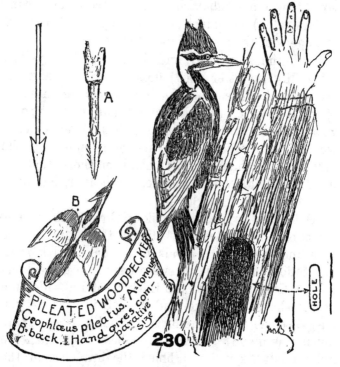

PILEATED WOODPECKER
Ceophlœus pileatus. A-tongue.
B-back. Hand gives com-
parative size

230

horns, or rubbing them exactly as a cow does on the tree in the pasture lot.

It may happen that in a beech wood you find a beech tree which has been gnawed and a great part of the bark eaten; the teeth marks are smaller than those of a beaver, and beaver do not go so far inland. What has been here?

Yes, you guessed right the first time. It was a porcupine. And here is a stick which we cut in the Maine woods; a porcupine has gnawed it one season and the wound has healed up and it has been gnawed again the second season.

The writer passed this same stick around among a class he had in Scout craft, composed of school teachers, Sunday School teachers, Y.M.C.A. men, slum workers and college professors; in the class there was a Chinaman and a negro. The writer asked the class if they noticed anything peculiar about the stick.

Only one of them did; it was but a stick to the rest. The one who did notice it said, "Chief, sir, this stick has been gnawed by some rat-like animal; but its teeth are much larger than any rat that I ever saw; the wounds on the plant have healed up and the animal has come back next season and gnawed it again."

Which one of those men do you think was the real scientist and used his brains to reason this out? It was not the college professor, but the colored man! In that class of about thirty bright men, city men, none of them had developed their power of observation sufficiently to know that that stick was not exactly like any other stick that they might find in a bunch of fagots or kindling wood.

On our walk along the wilderness trail recently, we found a log of wood, a rotten log which had been lately pulled apart. Now what did this? What object would any animal have in clawing that log apart? Of course it was not done just for fun. We looked closely. Yes, there had been an ants' nest in this log. What animal is there in the forest that is fond of ants' eggs? Here is where woods knowledge comes in play. You all know that the black bear dotes on ants' eggs.

Beyond this rotten log I am talking about there was a black spruce tree, still bleeding from fresh

231

RUFFED GROUSE
100% American
Bonasa umbellus

wounds in its bark, or skin, when the writer took the picture, showing where Bruin stood on his hind legs and clawed the tree. We know that Bruin stood upright because no bear could reach so high unless he stood upright.

Here is another stick, a piece of striped maple from which the bark has been stripped, not with the claws but with the teeth of some animal, and you, being a woodsman, know that the the moose are very fond of striped maple bark, and that the plant itself is often known as moosewood. Therefore you do not have to make three guesses to tell what animal did this.

WHAT YOU CAN DO NEAR HOME

But woodcraft can be studied near home, wherever there are trees and fields, wherever nature has a chance to crowd into our towns, cities, or suburbs, there will be found wild mice, birds, and not infrequently gray squirrels. All of these things live near my home in Greater New York City, and the boys around here trap numerous muskrats and occasionally mink.

Not long since, while visiting a neighbor, the writer noticed on the ground under a fir tree quite a number of little round balls which, upon examination, proved to consist of fur and the tiny bones of mice. What did this tell him? It said, as plainly as it could say, that some bird of prey was accustomed to roost in the fir tree, because birds of prey spit out the indigestible bones or fur of animals which they have swallowed, in the form of rounded masses about the size of big marbles, and these are called pellets.

Stepping back, the writer peered up among the branches of a fir tree and discovered not only one, but *seven* long-eared owls. And this was in the city of New York!

You can never tell what stories you can read of the lives and habits of our friends in fur and feathers until you try. Look about you and think hard, with the clear, reasoning head of a woodsman!

Maybe you will run across that splendid, gaudy, big woodpecker known as the pileated woodpecker, which digs chips out of the tree as big as beaver chips. He is a splendid and rare bird; you will find him in the pine forests. There are many of them around my woodcraft camp in Pike County, Pennsylvania. (Fig. 230.)

In the same neighborhood you are likely to run

232 SOLITARY SANDPIPER
Totanus solitarius

across that grand American bird, the ruffed grouse—find its tracks in the snow or find where it has dusted itself like a barnyard fowl by the side of the road (Fig. 231). While the writer was hunting moose with Mr. Fred Vreeland and Scout Joe Van Vleck, they stalked a ruffed grouse and got within five feet of it; the author then imitated the drumming of the grouse by beating on the ground with the palm of his hand. Scout Van Vleck and Mr. Vreeland had their cameras set and succeeded in photographing this bird in the act of drumming. I think these photographs are the only ones ever taken of a wild ruffed grouse drumming, and I am certain that very few people, even among hunters and woodsmen, have ever seen a grouse drumming. But by careful work this old cock became so accustomed to our presence that he would drum for us whenever the writer would beat the ground with the palm of his hand.

This experience alone was worth the trip to the Northern wilds. Any man who can shoot a gun can hit a moose. But it is a real privilege to watch a grouse on the old drumming log going through his strange ceremony. First he ruffs up all his feathers, then stands up as straight as possible, spreading his tail back of him on the log while he beats his body with his wings, moving them slowly at first, then gradually faster and faster until the eye is unable to follow the movement. This was really the best piece of stalking the writer ever accomplished.

Along the shore you will see the different shore birds, birds with long legs and the habit of bobbing up and down, like the solitary sandpiper (Fig. 232). In the last three figures the author has made the outline of the human hand to show the comparative size of the birds.

All of these creatures you will have to stalk carefully in order to get a good view of them. Especially is this true of the pileated woodpecker, but the joy of seeing them and the triumph experienced in stalking them successfully in order to get a good sight will amply repay you for your trouble and add immensely to the interest of a hike in the woods.

CHAPTER VIII

A COLLECTING HIKE
HOW TO BRING HOME AND KEEP
LIVE SPECIMENS

A Collecting Hike

Every real Scout, and for that matter every real boy, should be a nature lover. The cold spring bubbling up under the hill should be a delight to him, so also should the floating cranberry bog covered with sphagnum moss, young hackmatack trees, wild callow lillies, fringed purple orchids, pitcher plants, sundew, and all those thousands of interesting plants that flourish on a floating bog, and the creatures, frogs, turtles and salamanders that live among them. A Scout should love the brown path, the indistinct trail up the mountain and the creatures that live beside the trail and the birds in the bushes or trees overhead. If he cultivates a love of this kind he will cultivate something that will make him happy all his long life. I say long life because a love of nature gives one a long life.

The droning of the bees, the twitter of the birds, the whisper of the pines, the laughter of the brook, the gurgling of the spring, the creaking of saddle leather, the clinking of the bit and spur, the breathing of the broncho, the singing of ungreased wagon wheels, the crunching sound of the snow and the flopping of the snowshoe—why do we love to repeat these words?

The shrill whistle of the marmot high among the rocks; the screams of the eagle, the "who, who, who-who, who-ah!" of the barred owl, the whistling of the elk, the "woof woof" of the bear, the long-drawn howl of the timber wolf, the "yap-yap-yap" of the coyote, the uncanny grunting of the moose, the wild yell of the panther, the roar of the torrent, the crash-

ing thunder of the avalanche—what is there in these words that makes the blood tingle in one's veins?

It is the power of suggestion they possess. In them is the song of Mother Earth with the tang of the damp leaves under foot, the almond-like odor of twin flowers, the smell of pine needles, the view of vast expanses, the blue skies and towering clouds! The voicing of these words give us a magic carpet like that of "The Thief of Bagdad," which in imagination transports us to our old camping grounds. These words strike the fetters from our souls, set our spirits free, and though we may be writing in an attic; sitting on a high stool humped over a ledger; bending over our books at school, selling goods behind a ribbon counter, or papers on the street, it matters not, we forget these things and again become natural, normal, primal men and boys listening to Nature's great runes, odes, epics, lyrics, poems, ballads, and roundelays as sung by God's own bards, air, earth and water.

It was because these things appealed to John James Audubon, Henry David Thoreau, John Muir, John Burroughs and Theodore Roosevelt, that their names are now ones with which to conjure.

There is one absolutely necessary thing for an enjoyable hike, and that is an object. It is fun to go out to do one's scout stunt of fourteen miles in a day because we have an object in view. It is fun to take a hike to go afishing, to visit the Indian caves and hunt for specimens, and it is great fun to go on a hike to collect live specimens. To accomplish this, one must be a good stalker, and if we do catch the live specimens, we must have some means of carrying them home without injury to the specimens and last but not least, without injury to ourselves. Even an American white-footed mouse, which we find in the woods and the fields can bite one severely, but if you drop it in a handkerchief, gather up the end of the handerchief, you can carry it a long distance without injury to the mouse or to yourself. The same is true of the flying squirrel or even the gray squirrel, although you would need something larger than an ordinary pocket handkerchief for a gray squirrel.

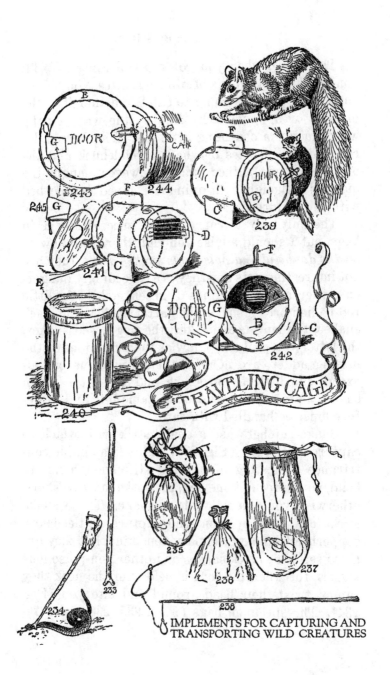

TRAVELING CAGE

IMPLEMENTS FOR CAPTURING AND
TRANSPORTING WILD CREATURES

Therefore, when you go on a collecting hike fill your pockets with bags of different sizes, you do not know what you are going to catch, whether it is the measles or a woodchuck. And by the way, a baby woodchuck is a charming little pet. When my children had the measles one had a woodchuck and the other a kitten, neither animal however, caught the measles although both animals romped on the bed with the children.

The only way to carry snakes successfully is in bags, but I should advise you right here and now to *let the doubtful and poisonous snakes alone,* they are not interesting pets and they are exceedingly dangerous, whereas the two kinds of green snakes, the little red-bellied brown snake, the garter snakes, the black snakes, the ring neck snakes, the hog-nosed snakes, the latter you probably know as the puff adder or the hissing adder, are none of them venomous but all except the little green snake and the little brown snake can give you an uncomfortable bite and therefore must be handled with care.

Snake catchers use a snake stick with which to capture their prey (Fig. 233). This is a simple contrivance consisting of a wand stiff enough not to bend, with a fork at one end, the forks must be short, otherwise you can not hold a snake. These snake sticks are used by men who capture rattlesnakes, copperheads and all the poisonous kind, but they are also useful for black snakes and other non-poisonous snakes, for when the fork is held over the neck they cannot twist their head around and bite you (Fig. 234). The specimen bags (Figs. 235, 236 and 237), can be made of unbleached muslin, they will occupy little room in your pockets until you have the live specimens in them.

Another useful instrument in capturing live creatures is a thin copper-wire slip noose (Fig. 238). This you can carry in your hat band and attach it to a rod or pole when you are on the hunting grounds. With it you can capture frogs, turtles and other live creatures, which will not fear the noose when it will be impossible for you to approach near enough to reach them with your hand. In using the copper slip noose be careful not to jerk it with much force for then you will cut your specimen in two as I told, earlier. Now that we have the implements with which to catch the animals, and the bags with which to transport them, we will proceed to build something more substantial in which to keep them at home or in camp.

KEEPING LIVE SPECIMENS

Some years ago I captured a beautiful little flying squirrel for my children. This was in Indiana, and when the time came to move to New York the youngsters insisted that we must take the flying squirrel with us, and so, with the help of a neighbor, we made a traveling box for him out of a tin box about five inches in diameter (Fig. 239). The tin box (Fig. 240), had a lid in which a round hole was cut, see dotted lines on the lid Figure 240, and a circular piece from a similar box, A, Figure 241, had a round hole put in it, and then was forced into the centre of the box where it fitted snugly and divided the interior

into two compartments, see A, Figure 241 and A,
Figure 242. The latter diagram shows an end view of
the box looking in at the door, B is a piece of tin
partly covering the door space, so as to make the
opening smaller and lessen the chance of escape of
the inmate when the door is opened. A is the division
in the middle of the box through the hole of which you
can see the bars D at the rear of the box, see Figure
241. Figures 243 and 244 show how the door is made,
and 245 shows the hinge, which is simply a piece of
tin bent over a short bit of wire. In the fold of the
bent tin the door is soldered so that one-half comes on
one side of the door and the other half upon the opposite side of the door, G, Figures 245, 243, 242 and 239.
The wire is soldered onto the rim E, Figure 240.
Opposite the hinge a bent wire is soldered onto the
door to fit over the staple, also made of a bent wire,
which is soldered onto the side of the can (Figs. 243
and 244). At the bottom of the box a piece of bent
tin, C, Figures 239 and 241, is bent up and soldered
onto the sides of the box, this is to prevent the can
from rolling when it is resting upon a table or the
floor. On the top of the box (Figs. 239, 241 and 242),
is soldered F, another piece of bent wire to serve
as a handle.

It is astonishing what a comfortable, fine traveling case this made, and as far as outward appearances was concerned, or inward appearances, as
the case may be, the flying squirrel was very happy
in its traveling box. In the back compartment with
the barred window we placed cotton, in the front
compartment next to the door we placed food and

drink, as the occasion required. Fanny Flying
Squirrel made the journey from Indiana to Flushing
in comfort, and for all I know to the contrary is still
living in the oak trees in old Flushing, Long Island,
because after keeping it a little while we allowed it
to escape.

Boxes, Cages and Dens for Our Pets

Can be easily made of wire mesh, such as you may
procure at any hardware store, make your pattern
of manila paper first, if you intend to make a real
serviceable and good looking cage use Figure 250.
design. A simple cylinder of wire mesh can be used
(Fig. 246) after end pieces are cut and fitted to it for
a receiving cage for the temporary confinement of
your pets. The advantage of this pattern is its sim-
plicity; bend a strip of wire mesh around until the
ends meet, then sew them together with thin wire or
a bit of picture wire, cut two pieces of mesh to fit
the ends and wire them in place and the trick is done.
The one I used all one summer had no doorway, but
one part of one end piece could be lifted open so that
I could thrust in my hand and arm or slip in
a specimen.

Figures 247 and 248 are two other simple forms.
Figure 249 shows a neat and simple cage made the
shape of a house, Figure 250 is the pattern for it, the
dotted lines show the places to fold; the open edges
are to be sewed together with wire as already
described. If you have any skill at all and use ordinary care you can make any one of these cages. The
only difficult part, I was going to say, is the door and

DETAILS OF HOME MADE CAGES

doorways, but difficult is too big a word for so simple
a piece of work, and we will paraphrase it by saying
the only part that will at all exercise your patience
will be the door and doorway.

Figure 256 shows the opening cut in the mesh for
the doorway; Figure 257 shows the piece cut out of
the opening of which we make the door. Figure 251
is a rough piece of tin, Figure 252 shows how to fold
the tin so as to do away with the rough edges. When
your tin is folded (T, Fig. 253), and of the right size
to fit the end of your door (T, Fig. 256), make holes
at the proper points by placing the folded tin on a
block of wood and driving a nail through wherever
you wish a hole to be. Figure 255 shows the shape
of the tin made to fit on the sides of the door, bend
it at the dotted lines where it is marked "bend here,"
slip it over the edges of the doorway as T is in Figure
256. This will make the door jams. It also makes the
doorway a little smaller, so that the door itself will
fit outside of it. T, Figure 257 shows the pieces of
tin before they are sewed onto the edges of the door.
The top T shows one that has already been sewed on
with a bit of wire. After the door is made hinge it
with two loops of wire on one side and fasten a hook
and staple of wire to the other side, as shown in
Figure 254. Figure 258 is still another form of cage,
it is one I made for some white-footed mice. I sewed
a tin bottom to this cage, and then sodded it with
grass sod, against the sides of the cage I wired a
last year's bird nest, in the birds nest the little white-
footed mice lived contentedly for some time, then to
my surprise they deserted the nest, destroyed it

and with the material made a nest under the sod, and in that nest I found some wee, little, hairless mice as blind as bats. They looked like miniature hippopotamuses.

With the wire screen and wire netting it requires but little trouble and care to make cages for all sorts of small creatures, anything from a full-grown wood-chuck to a butterfly, and thus you may have a miniature zoological garden at your camp, counsel room or home.

The neatness and natty appearance of the cages does not depend so much upon the skill of the work-man as it does upon the *care* he takes. I have almost reached a point where I am ready to substitute the word care for skill, because the most skillful men in the arts and sciences, as well as the trades, whom I have met, are the ones who do the most careful work, and the most successful keepers of pets are also the ones who are the most careful. Also, the ones who most enjoy a hike in the country, through the fields, or through the forests, are the ones who are the most careful about their outfitting and the most careful observers on the hikes. The late Langdon Gibson, who was with Peary on his Arctic Expedition and also went down the terrible rapids and canyon of the Colorado, and his brother Charles Dana Gibson the famous artist, and Mr. Frederick K. Vreeland, one of my counselors on the National Court of Honor, a famous sportsman, naturalist, and scientist, are the three men with whom I have had the most enjoyable boating and camping expeditions. Why? Because all three of them were careful observers. I knew

them all before they were famous. I hiked with the
Gibson boys before they had long trousers and I
camped with Mr. Vreeland before he was a Scout.
Now there is little doubt that the success of these
three famous men is due to their careful work and
their careful observation, and all three of them were
great nature lovers from their childhood to manhood.

CHAPTER IX

HOW TO BUILD A CANVAS CANOE
AND A DUG-OUT CANOE

The Canvas Canoe

It takes a red Indian all of thirty days to build a good birch bark canoe, and you had better allow fully that time to build yourself a canvas canoe, which after all is only a birch bark canoe on which white men have substituted canvas for the bark of the birch tree.

Material

The great problem which faces us in the construction of anything today is the question of material, but a good scout and a good woodcrafter must learn to use the material at hand. My old friend, the late Andrew J. Stone, 'way up in the far north where there are no trees, only shrubs, made himself the frame of a canoe by binding willow wands together and then tying on this frame a cover of waterproof cloth, which Colonel David Abercrombie had given him, to protect his specimens on his collecting trips. With this hastily constructed canoe he crossed a turbulent glacier stream. The boat was loaded with the skins and heads of mountain sheep, guns and ammunition, himself and a couple of Indians, but he made the crossing safely! In the Ohio and Mississippi Valleys the Indians used canoes hollowed out of logs, in spite of the fact that our modern illus-

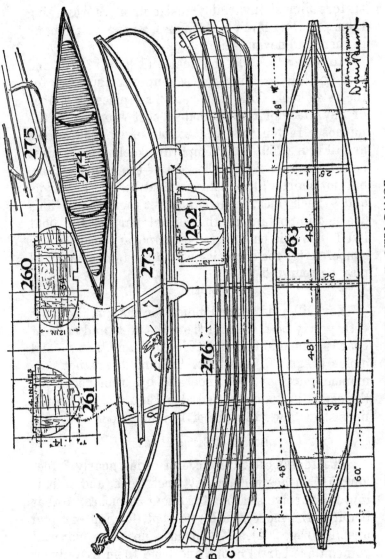

HOW TO MAKE YOUR OWN CANOE

trators almost invariably insist upon representing them paddling birch bark canoes, a type which many of them had never seen.

In order to build the boat and hold it firm and steady while so doing, lay a temporary support for the false keel. This may be a 2 x 4 piece of timber or any piece of timber that is stiff enough for the purpose; fasten this to a couple of wooden horses as in Figure 259. This temporary keel support must be a trifle longer than the keel of the canoe will be, but not shorter; for instance let it be 3 inches wide, and ½ inch thick, if you wish, but these dimensions are not important as this is not part of the boat itself. To this base fasten a temporary keel for the canoe. After the canoe is molded the temporary keel may be removed.

Molds

You will need several molds for shaping the craft —they may be fashioned from the odds and ends of boards—the middle mold (Fig. 260) and the two end molds (Figs. 261 and 262). The molds are not permanent parts of the canoe and are removed after the canoe is framed. See also Figure 263. Dotted lines show bow and stern of 16 foot canoe.

Bow and Stern Pieces

The Indians used a piece of cedar nearly 3 feet long, 1½ inches wide, and ½ inch thick, and split it into four or five sections for about 30 inches, so that it might the more readily be bent, leaving one end unsplit (Fig. 264). If you have no other material you can use barrel hoops and bend them by putting them into boiling water or pouring boiling water upon them and then lashing several of them together with copper wire. Or you can be still more crude and use the heads of barrels as shown in Figure 265. Or you may take straight-grained green elm, a piece a trifle less than 3 feet long, as wide as one's palm, and ½ inch thick, and bend it by fastening pieces of wire to each end as you would string a bow, with a double string, then make a tourniquet by putting a stick between the wires and twisting it until the tension of the twisted wire (Figs. 264 and 259) bends the elm. Remember that boiling water will always soften the wood so that it will bend more or less readily. Leave the stick and the twisted wire on until the wood is dry.

Ribs

Our canoe must have from forty to fifty ribs. These ribs should be split from the heart of a white cedar log, split with their flat sides (Fig. 266) parallel to the bark or outside of the billet of wood. Otherwise the ribs will be weak and liable to break when you try to bend them. The ribs will bend more readily with the heart side (Fig. 269A) for the inside of the rib. You may discard or throw away the sapwood and the slabs (Fig. 267), as they are unfit for our purpose. Each rib is 1½ inches thick and the breadth of your hand. The middle rib may be 4 inches wide.

If the white cedar is unobtainable, elm wood will answer, and it may usually be procured at an old fashioned blacksmith or wagon shop, if such exists

in your neighborhood; or you may use hickory for
the ribs. Whatever you use, let it be green wood and
used before it has time to season. The ribs may be
softened by putting them in boiling water or pouring
boiling water upon them. When you bend them, bend
them in pairs, two at a time, and hold them as shown
in Figure 270. I have seen a serviceable canoe made
with barrel hoops for ribs, but the craft, while light

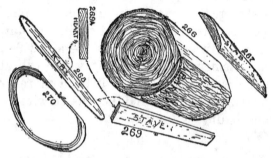

and useable, lacked the snappy, elegant appearance
which we love to see in a canvas canoe. The ribs
(Fig. 268) are made from the staves (Figs. 269 and
269A), which have been split from the heart of the
billet of green wood. They are each whittled down
by hand and smoothed with a knife to the shape and
form of the diagram (Fig. 268). They are very
important in shaping the canoe. The curve of the
ribs determine the depth and stability of the boat.

Gunwales

For gunwales (Fig. 271) use long strips that may
be procured from any of the carpenters who put
down hardwood floors. These strips are 2 inches
wide by ¼ inch thick. They may be of red cedar,

HOW TO BUILD A CANOE

259

272

271

261

265

spruce, ash, birch, or any wood available that will
not warp and which has no knots or blemishes in it.
These are to be fastened to the frame as shown in
Figure 276. The ends of the gunwales are made fast
to the stems, both bow and stern, and may be fastened
on with screws. The point is to
make them snug and secure. The
other strips are put temporarily in place
and evenly spaced between the gunwales
and the bottom of the boat. These strips
are used to give form to the ribs and may
be removed after they have served their
purpose.

The gunwales are the long pieces on
the top of the sides of the canoe. If the
strips are not firm enough tack two strips
together, one over the other, thus making
one piece of them ½ inch thick. If
necessary three or even four such pieces
may be fastened together until the gunwale is one inch thick, but in this
case do not put the extra pieces
on until after the canvas is fastened on the frame.
Fasten them firmly but temporarily to the frame
work and to the molds, and see that they fit neatly in
the offsets on top of the molds. Let the ends of the
gunwales meet at the stem and the stern, as shown by
Figures 271, 272 and 273; fasten the ends securely
and permanently to the stem pieces (Fig. 273).

The ribs are now put in place (Fig. 274). First
put the centre rib on the upper side of the temporary
keel (Fig. 275). Nail it securely to the false keel
but do not drive the nails home—leave enough

standing to make it easy to insert the claw of a
hammer beneath the head and remove it when all is
ready. Bend the ends of the ribs gently until they
fit inside the gunwale (Fig. 275). Nail the ends of
the ribs to the gunwales, using one inch galvanized
brads for the purpose. As soon as all the ribs are in
place, remove the side strips A, B and C, Figure 276.
In order to further stiffen your craft put a strip 2
inches wide and about 1¼ inches thick and long
enough to reach from stem to stern and be lap-
jointed to the stem and stern piece as was the false
keel (Figs. 264 and 271).

Now make fast the crossbars, of rock maple, if
it can be procured, if not, some other tough wood.
The dimensions of the crossbars are 2 inches by ⅞
inch, and long enough to fit the canoe (Figs. 274 and
277). Use an awl to make holes in the crossbars and
the gunwales and with copper wire lash these in place
just as the Indians did with roots on their birch bark
canoes. (Fig. 277.)

CANVAS

For a 15 foot canoe use No. 10 seamless cotton
canvas; for a canoe 16 feet or more use No. 8 seamless canvas, of sufficient width to cover the bottom
and sides of the canoe. Fold the canvas lengthwise
so as to find its exact centre and crease it like you
would your trousers. Lay the canvas on evenly the
length of the boat with the crease of centre-line along
the centre of the keel. With the assistance of a helper
pull it as taut as may be from stem to stern, and using
4 ounce tinned or copper tacks, tack the centre-line
to the stem and stern. If this has been done carefully the cloth will hang an equal length over each

side of the canoe. Set three or four tacks lightly along the centre of the bottom of the canoe, but do not drive the tacks down to their heads because they are only put there temporarily. Begin amidship and drive tacks lightly about 2 inches apart along the gunwale, say an inch below the top surface. After having tacked it for about 2 feet go to the other side of the boat, pull the cloth taut, and in the same manner tack about 3 feet. Continue this process first on one side and then the other until finished. While stretching the cloth work and knead it with your hand and fingers so as to thicken or "full" it where it would otherwise wrinkle; by doing this carefully it is possible to stretch the canvas smoothly over the frame without the necessity of cutting it. The cloth that extends beyond the frame may be brought over the gunwale and tacked along the inside. The canvas is now stretched on every part except on the bow and stern. With a pair of shears carefully slit the canvas from the outer edge of the bow and stern to within a half inch of the ends of the keel.

Fold the right-hand flap thus made at the left-hand end around the bow and stern and drawing tight, cut away the surplus canvas and glue the flap down. Heat powdered glue and water in a double boiler, apply a thin coat of glue with a paint brush; after the boat is painted and varnished there will be no danger of the glue softening. Next fold the left-hand flap over the right-hand side and glue it in a similar manner, trimming off the remaining cloth neatly. If there be any wrinkles the lightly set tacks can be removed and reset; if not, all tacks may now be driven home. Now that the canvas is all snug and stretched, tack on the other strips of gunwale over the canvas-covered pieces.

As far as building a canoe is concerned there is no way to "gyp" through, you've got to get down to work and build it. Charles Dana Gibson and his brother, the late Langdon Gibson, when they were of Scout age built themselves a canoe and took me out on its trial trip on old Flushing Bay. They paddled and sailed in that canoe from Flushing Bay to Newport, Rhode Island—and what these two lads did you can do if you knuckle down to it. If you've got the real soul of a scout in you it will be fun to work out the problems of canoe building and a delight to your soul when in the end you've turned out a beautiful Indian craft of your own make. As you sit back and look at it you may sing:

What is it that's making the old world go 'round?—
"WORK!" Tra la la, doodle dum dee,
What's keeping a lot of good folks above ground?—
"WORK!" Tra la la, Sally bring the tea.
Don't be in a flurry,
Oh, Gee!
You'r sleep old Turk—
Just sidestep old worry
With good, steady WORK!
With a fo, with a fiddle,
With a high diddle diddle,
Get busy!
Yo ho
Earn your prok!

How to Make a Dugout Canoe

Select a white wood tree, if possible, a spruce, red wood or pine will do. Let it be one with a long straight trunk free from knots and branches, cut some skids about six inches in diameter for the tree to fall upon so that the log may not rest on the ground (Fig. 278), and also so that it may be more easily handled. From trunk of the fallen tree cut a log about seventeen feet long, a shorter one will do but seventeen is a handy length. With an axe cut the bark off of the half which will be the bottom of the proposed canoe (Figs. 279, 280 and 283). Flatten the bottom a trifle, say 1½ feet wide, by scoring slightly and hewing a level strip from stem to stern. With a chalk string snap a line along the peeled sides of the log to mark the gunwales of the canoe, allowing about 17 inches for depth of canoe. If chalk will not mark on the wood, wet charcoal dust and cover the string with that.

Leaving about 2 feet at bow and stern begin to score by chopping notches along the top of the log down to the chalked line (Figs. 279 and 280). Next hew away the wood between the notches (Fig. 280 and 282). To save moving the log so often the bow and stern are sometimes shaped when the log is in the position of Figure 279.

The block of wood between notches can be mostly split off by first driving the axe at different points down to the chalk line and then using two wedges on each side of each block.

When all surplus wood is split or hewn away, begin to hollow out the inside, this requires careful

278

SCORING THE LOG

279

SCORING AND HEWING

280

282

HEWING THE
TOP OF THE LOG

281

work to prevent making splits or holes in the sides.
An adz is a useful tool for this work but a good
axeman needs no other tool than this axe. Amateurs
use an awl with which to make small holes in the sides
in these holes they drive slivers with blackened ends
so as to guide them when hollowing to log and keep

FELLING THE TREE
AND
PEELING THE BARK.

283

the side a uniform thickness. Figure 281 finished
dugout canoe.

Lee Boards for Open Canoes

A canoe, as a rule, has no keel, skeg or centre
board, consequently it has not the hold on the water
necessary for a sailing craft, and unless some pro-
vision is made to prevent, the wind will blow the boat
sideways or broadside over the water. Therefore, in
order that one may use sails with a canoe it is necessary to have lee boards, Figure 284 shows the canoe
with the lee boards attached. Above the boy's head

are the details of the lee board. A is the board, B is the thwart rod which fits across the top of the canoe, C, C and C are the thumb screw clamps which fasten the lee board thwarts to the gunnel of the canoe. In the left hand corner of the picture is a section view of the lee boards showing how the thumb screw clamps

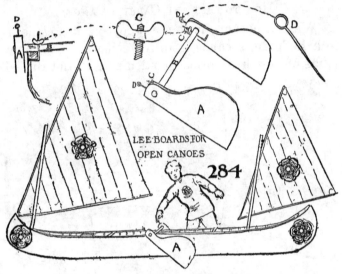

LEE BOARDS FOR OPEN CANOES

284

fasten onto the gunnel or a cleat put on the side of the canoe for that purpose. D, D, D are the pins which are dropped in holes bored through the top of the lee boards and the thwart stick. These pins should be attached with a chain to the lee board to prevent the embarrassment of losing them. When in place they nail, so to speak, the lee board to the thwart. By removing them one may take the two lee boards off the thwart stick and stow all three pieces away until vacation again requires their use.

CHAPTER X

HOW TO MAKE A PORTAGE. HOW TO HANDLE A CANOE. HOW TO ROW A BOAT. NAMES OF THE PARTS OF BOATS

How to Lift and Carry a Canoe

WHAT a broncho is to a cowboy, what a camel is to a Bedouin, a canoe is to a woodsman. In many parts of North America, particularly in the British

"Now twist your wrist
And bow you back,
And learn to turn
The good flapjack"

possessions, wilderness travel is done altogether by canoe. There are no trails in some sections, except the portages from one body of water to another, hence canoeing is a very important part of woodcraft, and a few hints upon the art are most appropriate for this book.

Figure 285 shows the seasoned woodsman at the end of a carry or portage; a portage or carry being a place where the voyager is compelled to pack his

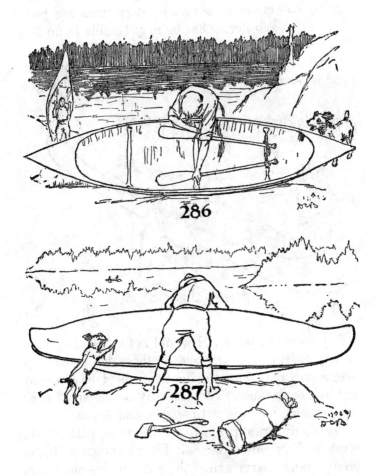

286

287

duffel on his back and his canoe on his shoulders in order that he may walk around some impassable rapids, waterfalls, or across country from one body of water to another. That he may be able to do this he must know how to pick up his canoe.

The only way to pick up a dug-out canoe is by placing somebody at each end of it and lifting it

bodily from the water. I would not advise any man or boy to try to carry one of these hollowed logs over a portage on his shoulders as one does a canvas or birch bark canoe. The best way to transport such cumbersome boats is with wagon and horse.

It is a different proposition, however, with a light birch bark or canvas canoe. I have known a strong young man to carry one of the latter on his shoulders over a five mile portage without once setting it down for a rest. On one occasion I saw three Indians each with a canoe over his head, carry them five miles

289

over the top of a mountain, in one place ascending a cliff on a ladder made of notched logs. If a man can lift a man's canoe, a big boy can lift a boy's canoe, and since some boys are as big and strong as men, I will tell them how to do it.

First lash the paddles onto the braces, as shown not in Figure 286 but 290. To pick up the canoe

stoop down and grasp the middle brace with both hands, the right reaching full length of arm, the left hand grasping it close to gunwale nearest your body; tip the canoe up (Figs. 286 and 287), lifting it clear off the ground. Then give it a heave lifting until it rests upon your knees, as it is in Figures 288 and 289. Next boost it up so that your right hand, holding the upper gunwale is extended above your head, as in Figure 290. Now shove the lower side up and lower the upper side of the canoe. Slip your head between the paddles as you twist the canoe around in position (Fig. 291). Unless you have a pad upon your

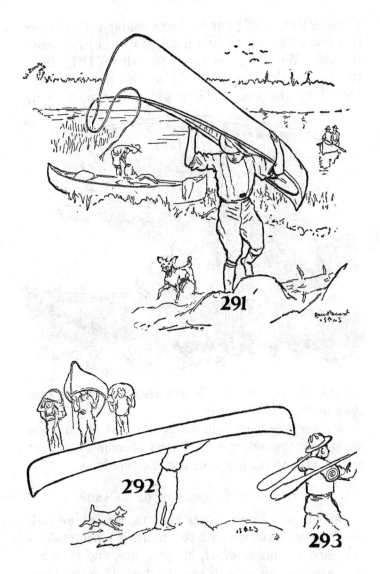

291

292

293

shoulders made of your coat or sweater rolled up, as in Figure 293, the paddle handles will not feel comfortable. When you are ready to walk off (Fig. 292), practically the whole weight of the canoe is supported by the two paddles which rest upon your

shoulders, and your hands are used more to balance than to support the canoe.

By keeping these diagrams in front of you and practising the act, you will soon become an expert and be able to handle your own canoe alone.

How to Get In and Out of a Canoe

A true woodsman treats his gun, his fishing rod, his axe, and his canoe with the greatest consideration and care, for his comfort, his pleasure, and even his life may depend upon these articles. One must not

step on the side of any boat when entering it, that
is the most certain way of upsetting, but an upset
for a woodsman would not be as serious as the injury
to his craft might be. A canoe, be it birch bark or
canvas, is very lightly built and it is not difficult for
one to put one's foot right through the side of the
canoe, the same is true of the shell boats used in
races. Therefore, whether the boat be light or heavy,
a canoe, rowboat, punt or scow, when you enter it
step exactly in the centre with the first foot (Figs.
294 and 295), and follow it with the second foot, then
seat yourself and all is well.

In the olden days, in the time of your great grandfathers, the keel-boatmen on the Mississippi and its
tributaries, used setting poles with which to pole
their cumbersome craft from New Orleans to Cairo,
St. Louis, Cincinnati, or Pittsburgh. To-day the setting pole is used by the canoeist both in poling up
and down rapids. In going down the rapids one
must use something with which to snub the canoe to
prevent it dashing ahead too rapidly and to enable
it to make quick turns. I have come through a series
of rapids using only the paddles, but the bowman's
paddle was literally worn out from jabbing it against
the bottom in order to snub the canoe. In a short
chapter like this, one cannot teach the perfect use of
the setting pole but one can indicate it so that the
reader may acquire the knowledge by practice.

Figure 296 shows the poles set and ready for a
heave. In this work one pole should always be
firmly resting upon the bottom. Figure 297 shows

the poise and the position when the polers are walking upstream hand over hand on the pole. Figure 298, the man in the bow is swinging for an opportunity to take another grip on his pole, while the man in the stern is holding the boat on its course by a firm purchase on the bottom with the lower end of his pole. I have seen a canoe poled by men stand-

ing up, which is a very ticklish operation, and only indulged in by the reckless or by experts. You pole upstream through the rapids, and you snub downstream through the rapids. Practice it where an upset will not be any more serious than a wetting, and when you become expert it is safe to say there will be no upsets.

If you upset a long distance from shore do not forget that a human head is a small object in the water, but an upset boat will almost certainly attract the attention of any sailor, fisherman or boating party. Therefore, stick to your craft. A capsized canoe will support at least four persons as long as they have the strength to cling to it. In case of upsetting beyond swimming distance to land, a single man or boy should stretch himself flat upon the bottom of the canoe, with arms and legs spread down over the tumblehome toward the submerged gunwales. He can thus lie in safety for hours till help arrives. When two persons are upset they should range themselves one on each side of the overturned

boat; and, with one hand grasping each other's wrists across the boat, use the other hand to cling to the keel or the gunwale. If the canoe should swamp, fill with water, and begin to sink, it should be turned over in the water. It is the air remaining under the inverted hull that gives the craft sufficient buoyancy to support weight.

Never overload a canoe. In one of the ordinary size—about 17 feet in length—three persons should be the maximum number at any time, and remember never to change seats in a canoe when out of your depth.

Rules and regulations as to what to do and how to do it in times of a catastrophe are alright and may often be the means of saving life, but they cannot always be complied with. When I upset in a storm on Long Island Sound, I did stay by the boat and was rescued by a steamer, but I could not get up on the overturned craft, the waves would not allow it (Fig. 299). It is possible that the conditions in the sketch may be exaggerated, but I have sketched it

as I remember it. The author does not mind owning up that on many occasions he has proved himself to be a chump, and on this particular day, chump-like, he thought he would see how much wind his little sailing canoe could stand. It was a canvas canoe but painted and varnished and rubbed and sandpapered and polished until the hull looked as though it was made of nothing less than brightly polished steel.

It was a lateen rigged boat; a bright turkey-red dragon was emblazoned on the foresail, while the jigger or dandy, aft, had a red spade in the centre of

it. The canoe was launched from the float of the old
Nerius Boat Club now a delapidated wreck of a house
without window lights, but in those days bursting
with life, laughter and song and crowded with
athletic young men, all of whom could handle any
kind of a boat in any kind of weather in any kind of

water. This particular day the wind was coming in
sullen gusts, the clouds were low and gray, the white
caps frosted the crests of the waves. And the
weather was unusually cold for that time of the year.

As soon as the sails were hoisted upon the canoe
she bounded away over the waves like a bucking
broncho. Gee, it was fine! She stood the waves all
right, and she stood the wind, but when the skipper

came about and started to sail home he discovered
that he had left the key to the centreboard in the
boathouse. The canoe had a fan centreboard which
let down by means of a key.

Not only did he find that the key to the centreboard was several miles away but he found that he
could not beat to windward with the canoe because
it made leeway; consequently it was blown sideways
out into Long Island Sound, and at last from sheer
exhaustion the Skipper was unable to move quickly
enough to shift the live ballast and went over backwards into the cold, slashing waters of the Sound.

Great blue crabs came floating lazily up alongside
of him and paddled around showing no fear. The
gulls sailed over within a few feet of his head, and
there was an uncanny feeling that both the crabs and
the gulls were counting on a square meal, which the
skipper was to furnish, but after an hour and a
half's soaking in the cold water and pelting rain he
fortunately was picked up by a passing steamboat.

Names of the Parts of Boats

Before we go any further upon the stream or
lake, we will stop a moment to point out the parts of
a boat, the names of these parts are just the same
for a canoe, for a flat-bottom skiff, or a round bottom
rowboat, and every boy and man on the sea coast
knows these names, but I have hundreds of readers
who do not know them, and I want to ask for the
patience of the old salts while I call the landlubber's
attention to Figure 300, which explains and names
the parts of the hand-propelled boat.

You will note that the sort of runner or keel piece
on the bottom of the boat is called a skeg, that the
rowlocks are composed of tholes or thole pins; that
the bow is the front and the stern is the back end of
the boat, that the seats are called thwarts, that the

starboard is the right-hand side of the boat when
one sits in the stern face to the bow, and that port is
the left-hand side of the boat, that the rope or chain
with which the boat is made fast is called the painter,
that the top edges of the sides of the boat are called
the gunwales, that the piece of wood to which the
sides are fastened at the bow of the boat is called the
stem—every boy ought to know this much about a
boat—and they DO now!

How to Row a Boat

Next let us give our attention to Figure 301; an eight oared shell has been selected for the illustration, because the young men rowing in the shell boat are more skilled than the ordinary oarsmen, and consequently give us a better example of how to

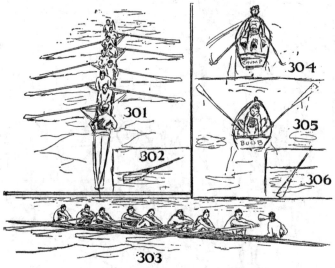

handle an oar. You will note that in Figure 303 they are all swinging forward preparatory to hitting the water with the blades of their oars. Now when they do hit they do not bury the oar blade and loom in the water, but only put the blade in so far (Fig. 302), that it may catch a good hold, so that when they swing back it will propel the boat forward.

We are not going into a scientific discourse on rowing; shell rowing does not belong to woodcraft, but every woodsman should know how to row a boat,

and Figures 304 and 305 show the poses of a landlubber in his attempt to row a skiff. You will note
that in Figure 304 he buries the oar away down and
in 305 he holds the blades away up in the air, so that
as the boat goes over the water, the oars flop like the
wings of a bird and each time he hits, the blade is
buried as shown in Figure 306. This is all wrong and
a waste of energy. The boat will go faster if he only
buries the blade of the oar as in Figure 301, and his
back will not be as lame. At any picnic or popular
resort you will see the boys and men rowing as in
Figures 304, 305 and 306, and at the first glance you
will know if they are landlubbers and unaccustomed
to a boat, but if you take any of the men from college
crews, or any of the old sailors and fishermen, you
will see that the oar blades do not go away up in the
air but just skip the top of the water as in Figures
301 and 303, and then only dip as in 302. Practice
rowing with these suggestions until you learn how,
and if you are going to go fishing or take a row for
pleasure in an ordinary boat, you will find that you
can row quietly in the proper manner so as not to
frighten your fish away by your splashing, and that
you will row with less effort, and consequently with
more enjoyment when you row properly than when
you alternately reach for the bottom of the sea
and the sky overhead.

A CATALOG OF SELECTED
DOVER BOOKS
IN ALL FIELDS OF INTEREST

A CATALOG OF SELECTED DOVER
BOOKS IN ALL FIELDS OF INTEREST

100 BEST-LOVED POEMS, Edited by Philip Smith. *"The Passionate Shepherd to His Love," "Shall I compare thee to a summer's day?" "Death, be not proud," "The Raven," "The Road Not Taken," plus works by Blake, Wordsworth, Byron, Shelley, Keats, many others. Includes 13 selections from the Common Core State Standards Initiative.* 112pp. 0-486-28553-7

1000 TURN-OF-THE-CENTURY HOUSES: With Illustrations and Floor Plans, Herbert C. Chivers. Reproduced from a rare edition, this showcase of homes ranges from cottages and bungalows to sprawling mansions. Each house is meticulously illustrated and accompanied by complete floor plans. 256pp. 0-486-45596-3

101 GREAT AMERICAN POEMS, Edited by The American Poetry & Literacy Project. Rich treasury of verse from the 19th and 20th centuries includes works by Edgar Allan Poe, Robert Frost, Walt Whitman, Langston Hughes, Emily Dickinson, T. S. Eliot, other notables. Includes 13 selections from the Common Core State Standards Initiative. 96pp. 0-486-40158-8

20TH-CENTURY FASHION ILLUSTRATION: The Feminine Ideal, Rosemary Torre. Introduction by Harold Koda. This captivating retrospective explores the social context of fashion with informative text and over 70 striking images. Profiles include flappers, glamour girls, flower children, and the modern obsession with celebrity styles. 176pp. 0-486-46963-8

3200 OLD-TIME CUTS AND ORNAMENTS, Edited by Blanche Cirker. Royalty-free pictures from 1909 French typography catalog: plants, animals, religious motifs, music, carriages, boats, sports, furniture, clothing; plus borders, banners, wreaths, and other ornaments. Over 3,200 black-and-white illustrations. 112pp. 0-486-41732-8

500 YEARS OF ILLUSTRATION: From Albrecht Dürer to Rockwell Kent, Howard Simon. Unrivaled treasury of art from the 1500s through the 1900s includes drawings by Goya, Hogarth, Dürer, Morris, Doré, Beardsley, others. Hundreds of illustrations, brief introductions. Ideal as reference and browsing book. 512pp. 0-486-48465-3

ABC BOOK OF EARLY AMERICANA, Eric Sloane. Artist and historian Eric Sloane presents a wondrous A-to-Z collection of American innovations, including hex signs, ear trumpets, popcorn, and rocking chairs. Illustrated, hand-lettered pages feature brief captions explaining objects' origins and uses. 64pp. 0-486-49808-5

ADVENTURES OF HUCKLEBERRY FINN, Mark Twain. Join Huck and Jim as their boyhood adventures along the Mississippi River lead them into a world of excitement, danger, and self-discovery. Humorous narrative, lyrical descriptions of the Mississippi valley, and memorable characters. 224pp. 0-486-28061-6

ALICE STARMORE'S BOOK OF FAIR ISLE KNITTING, Alice Starmore. A noted designer from the region of Scotland's Fair Isle explores the history and techniques of this distinctive, stranded-color knitting style and provides copious illustrated instructions for 14 original knitwear designs. 208pp. 0-486-47218-3

Browse over 10,000 books at www.doverpublications.com

ALICE'S ADVENTURES IN WONDERLAND, Lewis Carroll. Beloved classic about a little girl lost in a topsy-turvy land and her encounters with the White Rabbit, March Hare, Mad Hatter, Cheshire Cat, and other delightfully improbable characters. 42 illustrations by Sir John Tenniel. A selection of the Common Core State Standards Initiative. 96pp. 0-486-27543-4

AMERICAN BALLADS AND FOLK SONGS, John A. Lomax and Alan Lomax. Music and lyrics for over 200 songs. *John Henry, Goin' Home, Little Brown Jug, Alabama-Bound, Black Betty, The Hammer Song, Jesse James, Down in the Valley, The Ballad of Davy Crockett,* and many more. 672pp. 0-486-28276-7

AMERICAN LOCOMOTIVES IN HISTORIC PHOTOGRAPHS: 1858 to 1949, Ron Ziel. A rare collection of 126 meticulously detailed official photographs, called "builder portraits," majestically chronicle the rise of steam locomotive power in America. Introduction. Detailed captions. 140pp. 0-486-27393-8

ANIMALS: 1,419 Copyright-Free Illustrations of Mammals, Birds, Fish, Insects, etc, Selected by Jim Harter. Selected for its visual impact and ease of use, this outstanding collection of wood engravings presents over 1,000 species of animals in extremely lifelike poses. Includes mammals, birds, reptiles, amphibians, fish, insects, and other invertebrates. 284pp. 0-486-23766-4

THE ANNOTATED INNOCENCE OF FATHER BROWN, G. K. Chesterton. Twelve of the popular Father Brown mysteries appear in this copiously annotated edition. Includes "The Blue Cross," "The Hammer of God," "The Eye of Apollo," and more. 352pp. 0-486-29859-0

ANTIGONE, Sophocles. Filled with passionate speeches and sensitive probing of moral and philosophical issues, this powerful and often-performed Greek drama reveals the grim fate that befalls the children of Oedipus. Footnotes. 64pp. 0-486-27804-2

ART FORMS IN NATURE, Ernst Haeckel. Multitude of strangely beautiful natural forms: Radiolaria, Foraminifera, Ciliata, diatoms, calcareous sponges, Tubulariidae, Siphonophora, Semaeostomeae, star corals, starfishes, much more. All images in black and white. 100pp. 0-486-22987-4

THE ART OF WAR, Sun Tzu. Widely regarded as "The Oldest Military Treatise in the World," this landmark work covers principles of strategy, tactics, maneuvering, communication, and supplies; the use of terrain, fire, and the seasons of the year; much more. 96pp. 0-486-42557-6

THE ARTHUR RACKHAM TREASURY: 86 Full-Color Illustrations, Arthur Rackham. Selected and Edited by Jeff A. Menges. A stunning treasury of 86 full-page plates span the famed English artist's career, from *Rip Van Winkle* (1905) to masterworks such as *Undine, A Midsummer Night's Dream,* and *Wind in the Willows* (1939). 96pp. 0-486-44685-9

THE AUTHENTIC GILBERT & SULLIVAN SONGBOOK, W. S. Gilbert and A. S. Sullivan. The most comprehensive collection available, this songbook includes selections from every one of Gilbert and Sullivan's light operas. Ninety-two numbers are presented uncut and unedited, and in their original keys. 410pp. 0-486-23482-7

THE AUTOCRAT OF THE BREAKFAST-TABLE, Oliver Wendell Holmes. Witty, easy-to-read philosophical essays, written by the poet, essayist, and professor. Holmes drew upon his experiences as a resident of a New England boardinghouse to add color and humor to these reflections. 240pp. 0-486-79028-2

THE AWAKENING, Kate Chopin. First published in 1899, this controversial novel of a New Orleans wife's search for love outside a stifling marriage shocked readers. Today, it remains a first-rate narrative with superb characterization. New introductory note. 128pp. 0-486-27786-0

BASEBALL IS . . .: Defining the National Pastime, Edited by Paul Dickson. Wisecracking, philosophical, nostalgic, and entertaining, these hundreds of quips and observations by players, their wives, managers, authors, and others cover every aspect of our national pastime. It's a great any-occasion gift for fans! 256pp.　　0-486-48209-X

BEETHOVEN'S LETTERS, Ludwig van Beethoven. Edited by Dr. A. C. Kalischer. Features 457 letters to fellow musicians, friends, greats, patrons, and literary men. Reveals musical thoughts, quirks of personality, insights, and daily events. Includes 15 plates. 410pp.　　0-486-22769-3

BOUND & DETERMINED: A Visual History of Corsets, 1850–1960, Kristina Seleshanko. This revealing history of corsetry ranges from the 19th through the mid-20th centuries to show how simple laced bodices developed into corsets of cane, whalebone, and steel. Lavish illustrations include line drawings and photographs. 128pp.
0-486-47892-0

THE BUILDING OF MANHATTAN, Written and Illustrated by Donald A. Mackay. Meticulously accurate line drawings and fascinating text explain construction above and below ground, including excavating subway lines and building bridges and skyscrapers. Hundreds of illustrations reveal intricate details of construction techniques. A selection of the Common Core State Standards Initiative. 160pp.　　0-486-47317-1

THE BUNGALOW BOOK: Floor Plans and Photos of 112 Houses, 1910, Henry L. Wilson. Here are 112 of the most popular and economic blueprints of the early 20th century — plus an illustration or photograph of each completed house. A wonderful time capsule that still offers a wealth of valuable insights. 160pp.　　0-486-45104-6

THE CALL OF THE WILD, Jack London. A classic novel of adventure, drawn from London's own experiences as a Klondike adventurer, relating the story of a heroic dog caught in the brutal life of the Alaska Gold Rush. Note. 64pp.　　0-486-26472-6

CANDIDE, Voltaire. Edited by Francois-Marie Arouet. One of the world's great satires since its first publication in 1759. Witty, caustic skewering of romance, science, philosophy, religion, government — nearly all human ideals and institutions. A selection of the Common Core State Standards Initiative. 112pp.　　0-486-26689-3

THE CARTOON HISTORY OF TIME, Kate Charlesworth and John Gribbin. Cartoon characters explain cosmology, quantum physics, and other concepts covered by Stephen Hawking's *A Brief History of Time.* Humorous graphic novel–style treatment, perfect for young readers and curious folk of all ages. 64pp.　　0-486-49097-1

THE CHERRY ORCHARD, Anton Chekhov. Classic of world drama concerns passing of semifeudal order in turn-of-the-century Russia, symbolized in the sale of the cherry orchard owned by Madame Ranevskaya. Showcases Chekhov's rich sensitivities as an observer of human nature. 64pp.　　0-486-26682-6

A CHRISTMAS CAROL, Charles Dickens. This engrossing tale relates Ebenezer Scrooge's ghostly journeys through Christmases past, present, and future and his ultimate transformation from a harsh and grasping old miser to a charitable and compassionate human being. 80pp.　　0-486-26865-9

COMMON SENSE, Thomas Paine. First published in January of 1776, this highly influential landmark document clearly and persuasively argued for American separation from Great Britain and paved the way for the Declaration of Independence. A selection of the Common Core State Standards Initiative. 64pp.　　0-486-29602-4

THE COMPLETE SHORT STORIES OF OSCAR WILDE, Oscar Wilde. Complete texts of "The Happy Prince and Other Tales," "A House of Pomegranates," "Lord Arthur Savile's Crime and Other Stories," "Poems in Prose," and "The Portrait of Mr. W. H." 208pp.　　0-486-45216-6

Browse over 10,000 books at www.doverpublications.com

COMPLETE SONNETS, William Shakespeare. Over 150 exquisite poems deal with love, friendship, the tyranny of time, beauty's evanescence, death, and other themes in language of remarkable power, precision, and beauty. Glossary of archaic terms. Includes a selection from the Common Core State Standards Initiative. 80pp.   0-486-26686-9

THE COUNT OF MONTE CRISTO: Abridged Edition, Alexandre Dumas. Falsely accused of treason, Edmond Dantès is imprisoned in the bleak Chateau d'If. After a hair-raising escape, he launches an elaborate plot to extract a bitter revenge against those who betrayed him. 448pp.   0-486-45643-9

CRAFTSMAN BUNGALOWS: 59 Homes from "The Craftsman," Edited by Gustav Stickley. Best and most attractive designs from the Arts and Crafts Movement publication from 1903 to 1916 includes sketches, photographs of homes, floor plans, and descriptive text. 128pp.   0-486-25829-7

CRIME AND PUNISHMENT, Fyodor Dostoyevsky. Translated by Constance Garnett. Supreme masterpiece tells the story of Raskolnikov, a student tormented by his own thoughts after he murders an old woman. Overwhelmed by guilt and terror, he confesses and goes to prison. A selection of the Common Core State Standards Initiative. 448pp.   0-486-41587-2

CYRANO DE BERGERAC, Edmond Rostand. A quarrelsome, hot-tempered, and unattractive swordsman falls hopelessly in love with a beautiful woman and woos her for a handsome but slow-witted suitor. A witty and eloquent drama. 144pp.   0-486-41119-2

DANIEL BOONE'S OWN STORY & THE ADVENTURES OF DANIEL BOONE, Daniel Boone and Francis Lister Hawks. This two-part tale features reminiscences in the legendary frontiersman's own words and a profile of his entire life, with exciting accounts of blazing the Wilderness Road and serving as a militiaman during the Revolutionary War. 128pp.   0-486-47690-1

THE DECLARATION OF INDEPENDENCE AND OTHER GREAT DOCUMENTS OF AMERICAN HISTORY: 1775-1865, Edited by John Grafton. Thirteen compelling and influential documents: Henry's "Give Me Liberty or Give Me Death," Declaration of Independence, The Constitution, Washington's First Inaugural Address, The Monroe Doctrine, The Emancipation Proclamation, Gettysburg Address, more. Includes 3 selections from the Common Core State Standards Initiative. 64pp.   0-486-41124-9

A DOLL'S HOUSE, Henrik Ibsen. Ibsen's best-known play displays his genius for realistic prose drama. An expression of women's rights, the play climaxes when the central character, Nora, rejects a smothering marriage and life in "a doll's house." A selection of the Common Core State Standards Initiative. 80pp.   0-486-27062-9

DOOMED SHIPS: Great Ocean Liner Disasters, William H. Miller, Jr. Nearly 200 photographs, many from private collections, highlight tales of some of the vessels whose pleasure cruises ended in catastrophe: the *Morro Castle, Normandie, Andrea Doria, Europa,* and many others. 128pp.   0-486-45366-9

THE DORÉ BIBLE ILLUSTRATIONS, Gustave Doré. Detailed plates from the Bible: the Creation scenes, Adam and Eve, horrifying visions of the Flood, the battle sequences with their monumental crowds, depictions of the life of Jesus, 241 plates in all. 241pp.   0-486-23004-X

DUBLINERS, James Joyce. A fine and accessible introduction to the work of one of the 20th century's most influential writers, this collection features 15 tales, including a masterpiece of the short-story genre, "The Dead." 160pp.   0-486-26870-5

THE EARLY SCIENCE FICTION OF PHILIP K. DICK, Philip K. Dick. This anthology presents short stories and novellas that originally appeared in pulp magazines of the early 1950s, including "The Variable Man," "Second Variety," "Beyond the Door," "The Defenders," and more. 272pp.   0-486-49733-X

Browse over 10,000 books at www.doverpublications.com

THE EARLY SHORT STORIES OF F. SCOTT FITZGERALD, F. Scott Fitzgerald. These tales offer insights into many themes, characters, and techniques that emerged in Fitzgerald's later works. Selections include "The Curious Case of Benjamin Button," "Babes in the Woods," and a dozen others. 256pp. 0-486-79465-2

EASY BUTTERFLY ORIGAMI, Tammy Yee. Thirty full-color designs to fold include simple instructions and fun facts about each species. Patterns are perforated for easy removal and offer accurate portrayals of variations in insects' top and bottom sides. 64pp. 0-486-78457-6

EASY SPANISH PHRASE BOOK NEW EDITION: Over 700 Phrases for Everyday Use, Pablo Garcia Loaeza, Ph.D. Up-to-date volume, organized for quick access to phrases related to greetings, transportation, shopping, emergencies, other common circumstances. Over 700 entries include terms for modern telecommunications, idioms, slang. Phonetic pronunciations accompany phrases. 96pp. 0-486-49905-7

EINSTEIN'S ESSAYS IN SCIENCE, Albert Einstein. Speeches and essays in accessible, everyday language profile influential physicists such as Niels Bohr and Isaac Newton. They also explore areas of physics to which the author made major contributions. 128pp. 0-486-47011-3

EL DORADO: Further Adventures of the Scarlet Pimpernel, Baroness Orczy. A popular sequel to *The Scarlet Pimpernel*, this suspenseful story recounts the Pimpernel's attempts to rescue the Dauphin from imprisonment during the French Revolution. An irresistible blend of intrigue, period detail, and vibrant characterizations. 352pp. 0-486-44026-5

ELEGANT SMALL HOMES OF THE TWENTIES: 99 Designs from a Competition, Chicago Tribune. Nearly 100 designs for five- and six-room houses feature New England and Southern colonials, Normandy cottages, stately Italianate dwellings, and other fascinating snapshots of American domestic architecture of the 1920s. 112pp. 0-486-46910-7

THE ELUSIVE PIMPERNEL, Baroness Orczy. Robespierre's revolutionaries find their wicked schemes thwarted by the heroic Pimpernel — Sir Percival Blakeney. In this thrilling sequel, Chauvelin devises a plot to eliminate the Pimpernel and his wife. 272pp. 0-486-45464-9

ERIC SLOANE'S WEATHER BOOK, Eric Sloane. A beautifully illustrated book of enlightening lore for outdoorsmen, farmers, sailors, and anyone who has ever wondered whether to take an umbrella when leaving the house. 87 illustrations. 96pp. 0-486-44357-4

ETHAN FROME, Edith Wharton. Classic story of wasted lives, set against a bleak New England background. Superbly delineated characters in a hauntingly grim tale of thwarted love. Considered by many to be Wharton's masterpiece. 96pp. 0-486-26690-7

THE FEDERALIST PAPERS, Alexander Hamilton, James Madison, John Jay. A collection of 85 articles and essays that were initially published anonymously in New York newspapers in 1787–1788, this volume reflects the intentions of the Constitution's framers and ratifiers. 448pp. 0-486-49636-8

FINDING YOUR WAY WITHOUT MAP OR COMPASS, Harold Gatty. Useful, instructive manual shows would-be explorers, hikers, bikers, scouts, sailors, and survivalists how to find their way outdoors by observing animals, weather patterns, shifting sands, and other elements of nature. 288pp. 0-486-40613-X

FIRST SPANISH READER: A Beginner's Dual-Language Book, Edited by Angel Flores. Delightful stories, other material based on works of Don Juan Manuel, Luis Taboada, Ricardo Palma, other noted writers. Complete faithful English translations on facing pages. Exercises. 176pp. 0-486-25810-6

FIVE ACRES AND INDEPENDENCE, M. G. Kains. This classic of the back-to-the-land movement is packed with solid, timeless information. Written by a renowned horticulturist, it has taught generations how to make their land self-sufficient. 95 figures. 397pp. 0-486-20974-1

FLATLAND: A Romance of Many Dimensions, Edwin A. Abbott. Classic of science (and mathematical) fiction — charmingly illustrated by the author — describes the adventures of A. Square, a resident of Flatland, in Spaceland (three dimensions), Lineland (one dimension), and Pointland (no dimensions). 96pp. 0-486-27263-X

FRANKENSTEIN, Mary Shelley. The story of Victor Frankenstein's monstrous creation and the havoc it caused has enthralled generations of readers and inspired countless writers of horror and suspense. With the author's own 1831 introduction. 176pp. 0-486-28211-2

THE GARGOYLE BOOK: 572 Examples from Gothic Architecture, Lester Burbank Bridaham. Dispelling the conventional wisdom that French Gothic architectural flourishes were born of despair or gloom, Bridaham reveals the whimsical nature of these creations and the ingenious artisans who made them. 572 illustrations. 224pp. 0-486-44754-5

THE GIFT OF THE MAGI AND OTHER SHORT STORIES, O. Henry. Sixteen captivating stories by one of America's most popular storytellers. Included are such classics as "The Gift of the Magi," "The Last Leaf," and "The Ransom of Red Chief." Publisher's Note. A selection of the Common Core State Standards Initiative. 96pp. 0-486-27061-0

THE GÖDELIAN PUZZLE BOOK: Puzzles, Paradoxes and Proofs, Raymond M. Smullyan. These logic puzzles provide entertaining variations on Gödel's incompleteness theorems, offering ingenious challenges related to infinity, truth and provability, undecidability, and other concepts. No background in formal logic is necessary. 288pp. 0-486-49705-4

THE GOETHE TREASURY: Selected Prose and Poetry, Johann Wolfgang von Goethe. Edited, Selected, and with an Introduction by Thomas Mann. In addition to his lyric poetry, Goethe wrote travel sketches, autobiographical studies, essays, letters, and proverbs in rhyme and prose. This collection presents outstanding examples from each genre. 368pp. 0-486-44780-4

GREAT EXPECTATIONS, Charles Dickens. Orphaned Pip is apprenticed to the dirty work of the forge but dreams of becoming a gentleman — and one day finds himself in possession of "great expectations." Dickens' finest novel. 384pp. 0-486-41586-4

GREAT ILLUSTRATIONS BY N. C. WYETH, N. C. Wyeth. Edited and with an Introduction by Jeff A. Menges. This full-color collection focuses on the artist's early and most popular illustrations, featuring more than 100 images from *The Mysterious Stranger, Robin Hood, Robinson Crusoe, The Boy's King Arthur,* and other classics. 128pp. 0-486-47295-7

HAMLET, William Shakespeare. The quintessential Shakespearean tragedy, whose highly charged confrontations and anguished soliloquies probe depths of human feeling rarely sounded in any art. Reprinted from an authoritative British edition complete with illuminating footnotes. A selection of the Common Core State Standards Initiative. 128pp. 0-486-27278-8

THE HAUNTED HOUSE, Charles Dickens. A Yuletide gathering in an eerie country retreat provides the backdrop for Dickens and his friends — including Elizabeth Gaskell and Wilkie Collins — who take turns spinning supernatural yarns. 144pp. 0-486-46309-5

THE HEADS OF CERBERUS, Francis Stevens. Illustrated by Ric Binkley. A trio of time-travelers land in Philadelphia's brutal totalitarian state of 2118. Loaded with action and humor, this 1919 classic was the first alternate-world fantasy. "A much-sought rarity." — *Analog.* 192pp. 0-486-79026-6

HEART OF DARKNESS, Joseph Conrad. Dark allegory of a journey up the Congo River and the narrator's encounter with the mysterious Mr. Kurtz. Masterly blend of adventure, character study, psychological penetration. For many, Conrad's finest, most enigmatic story. 80pp. 0-486-26464-5

HISTORIC COSTUMES AND HOW TO MAKE THEM, Mary Fernald and E. Shenton. Practical, informative guidebook shows how to create everything from short tunics worn by Saxon men in the fifth century to a lady's bustle dress of the late 1800s. 81 illustrations. 176pp. 0-486-44906-8

THE HOUND OF THE BASKERVILLES, Sir Arthur Conan Doyle. A deadly curse in the form of a legendary ferocious beast continues to claim its victims from the Baskerville family until Holmes and Watson intervene. Often called the best detective story ever written. 128pp. 0-486-28214-7

THE HOUSE BEHIND THE CEDARS, Charles W. Chesnutt. Originally published in 1900, this groundbreaking novel by a distinguished African-American author recounts the drama of a brother and sister who "pass for white" during the dangerous days of Reconstruction. 208pp. 0-486-46144-0

HOW THE OTHER HALF LIVES, Jacob Riis. This famous journalistic record of the filth and degradation of New York's slums at the turn of the 20th century is a classic in social thought and of early American photography. Over 100 photographs. 256pp. 0-486-22012-5

HOW TO DRAW NEARLY EVERYTHING, Victor Perard. Beginners of all ages can learn to draw figures, faces, landscapes, trees, flowers, and animals of all kinds. Well-illustrated guide offers suggestions for pencil, pen, and brush techniques plus composition, shading, and perspective. 160pp. 0-486-49848-4

HOW TO MAKE SUPER POP-UPS, Joan Irvine. Illustrated by Linda Hendry. Super pop-ups extend the element of surprise with three-dimensional designs that slide, turn, spring, and snap. More than 30 patterns and 475 illustrations include cards, stage props, and school projects. 96pp. 0-486-46589-6

THE IMITATION OF CHRIST, Thomas à Kempis. Translated by Aloysius Croft and Harold Bolton. This religious classic has brought understanding and comfort to millions for centuries. Written in a candid and conversational style, the topics include liberation from worldly inclinations, preparation and consolations of prayer, and eucharistic communion. 160pp. 0-486-43185-1

THE IMPORTANCE OF BEING EARNEST, Oscar Wilde. Wilde's witty and buoyant comedy of manners, filled with some of literature's most famous epigrams, reprinted from an authoritative British edition. Considered Wilde's most perfect work. A selection of the Common Core State Standards Initiative. 64pp. 0-486-26478-5

THE INFERNO, Dante Alighieri. Translated and with notes by Henry Wadsworth Longfellow. The first stop on Dante's famous journey from Hell to Purgatory to Paradise, this 14th-century allegorical poem blends vivid and shocking imagery with graceful lyricism. Translated by the beloved 19th-century poet, Henry Wadsworth Longfellow. 256pp. 0-486-44288-8

JANE EYRE, Charlotte Brontë. Written in 1847, *Jane Eyre* tells the tale of an orphan girl's progress from the custody of cruel relatives to an oppressive boarding school and its culmination in a troubled career as a governess. A selection of the Common Core State Standards Initiative. 448pp. 0-486-42449-9

JAPANESE WOODBLOCK BIRD PRINTS, Numata Kashū. These lifelike images of birds and flowers first appeared in a now-rare 1883 portfolio. A magnificent reproduction of a 1938 facsimile of the original publication, this exquisite edition features 150 color illustrations. 160pp. 0-486-47050-4

Browse over 10,000 books at www.doverpublications.com

JULIUS CAESAR, William Shakespeare. Great tragedy based on Plutarch's account of the lives of Brutus, Julius Caesar, and Mark Antony. Evil plotting, ringing oratory, high tragedy with Shakespeare's incomparable insight, dramatic power. Explanatory footnotes. 96pp. 0-486-26876-4

THE JUNGLE, Upton Sinclair. 1906 bestseller shockingly reveals intolerable labor practices and working conditions in the Chicago stockyards as it tells the grim story of a Slavic family that emigrates to America full of optimism but soon faces despair. 304pp. 0-486-41923-1

JUST WHAT THE DOCTOR DISORDERED: Early Writings and Cartoons of Dr. Seuss, Dr. Seuss. Edited and with an Introduction by Rick Marschall. The Doctor's visual hilarity, nonsense language, and offbeat sense of humor illuminate this compilation of items from his early career, created for periodicals such as *Judge, Life, College Humor,* and *Liberty.* 144pp. 0-486-49846-8

KING LEAR, William Shakespeare. Powerful tragedy of an aging king, betrayed by his daughters, robbed of his kingdom, descending into madness. Perhaps the bleakest of Shakespeare's tragic dramas, complete with explanatory footnotes. 144pp. 0-486-28058-6

KNITTING FOR ANARCHISTS: The What, Why and How of Knitting, Anna Zilboorg. Every knitter takes a different approach, and this revolutionary guide encourages experimentation and self-expression. Suitable for active knitters and beginners alike, it offers illustrated patterns for sweaters, pullovers, and cardigans. 160pp. 0-486-79466-0

THE LADY OR THE TIGER?: and Other Logic Puzzles, Raymond M. Smullyan. Created by a renowned puzzle master, these whimsically themed challenges involve paradoxes about probability, time, and change; metapuzzles; and self-referentiality. Nineteen chapters advance in difficulty from relatively simple to highly complex. 1982 edition. 240pp. 0-486-47027-X

LEAVES OF GRASS: The Original 1855 Edition, Walt Whitman. Whitman's immortal collection includes some of the greatest poems of modern times, including his masterpiece, "Song of Myself." Shattering standard conventions, it stands as an unabashed celebration of body and nature. 128pp. 0-486-45676-5

LES MISÉRABLES, Victor Hugo. Translated by Charles E. Wilbour. Abridged by James K. Robinson. A convict's heroic struggle for justice and redemption plays out against a fiery backdrop of the Napoleonic wars. This edition features the excellent original translation and a sensitive abridgment. 304pp. 0-486-45789-3

LIGHT FOR THE ARTIST, Ted Seth Jacobs. Intermediate and advanced art students receive a broad vocabulary of effects with this in-depth study of light. Diagrams and paintings illustrate applications of principles to figure, still life, and landscape paintings. 144pp. 0-486-49304-0

LILITH: A Romance, George MacDonald. In this novel by the father of fantasy literature, a man travels through time to meet Adam and Eve and to explore humanity's fall from grace and ultimate redemption. 240pp. 0-486-46818-6

LINE: An Art Study, Edmund J. Sullivan. Written by a noted artist and teacher, this well-illustrated guide introduces the basics of line drawing. Topics include third and fourth dimensions, formal perspective, shade and shadow, figure drawing, and other essentials. 208pp. 0-486-79484-9

THE LODGER, Marie Belloc Lowndes. Acclaimed by *The New York Times* as "one of the best suspense novels ever written," this novel recounts an English couple's doubts about their boarder, whom they suspect of being a serial killer. 240pp. 0-486-78809-1